MW01165262

A Test of Commitment: 15 Challenges to Stimulate Your Devotion to Christ

Brian Johnston

Published by Hayes Press, 2016.

Published by

HAYES PRESS CHRISTIAN RESOURCES

The Barn, Flaxlands

Royal Wootton Bassett

Swindon, SN4 8DY

United Kingdom

www.hayespress.org

If you enjoyed reading this book and/or others in the series, we would really appreciate it if you could just take a couple of minutes to leave a brief review where you downloaded or purchased this book.

As a thank-you for purchasing this book, please help yourself to a free download of "Healthy Churches – God's Bible Blueprint For Growth" by Brian Johnston in the Search For Truth Series:

Amazon.com: http://amzn.to/1FuoN5l

Amazon.co.uk: http://amzn.to/1HTSize

TABLE OF CONTENTS

CHAPTER ONE: A GLASS OF WINE
(JEREMIAH)

As a man walked home one day, he found a wallet someone had lost in the street. He picked it up and searched it for identification in order to be able to contact its owner. But he only found three dollars and a crumpled letter that looked as if it'd been in there for years. The envelope was worn and almost the only thing that remained legible was the return address. Then he saw the date: 1924. The letter had been written almost sixty years earlier! It was written in a girl's handwriting to someone whose name appeared to be Michael, whom it seemed she was never to see again, because her mother had said their friendship was to stop. She was writing to say she'd still always love him, and signed off as Hannah.

It was a beautiful letter, but there was no way to identify the owner of the wallet, except for the name Michael. But, wait, wasn't there just one lead? For Hannah had put a return address! The telephone exchange confirmed there was a phone listing for Hannah's return address on the envelope, and the supervisor said as a courtesy, she'd call the number, and explain the situation. The woman on the other end of the line said they'd bought their house from a family who did have a daughter named Hannah - but that was thirty years ago.

But then she added that they'd kept in touch and she happened to know that Hannah had placed her mother in a certain nursing home some years ago. Well, this in turn led to another phone call (this time to the nursing home), during which it was explained that the old lady had passed away some years ago

- but the nursing home did have a phone number for where the daughter might be living. Phoning that number next, revealed the fact that Hannah herself was now living in a nursing home! And so it was that the finder of the wallet finally came to call the nursing home in which Hannah was supposed to be living – to be told "Yes, Hannah is staying with us."

It was by now already 10 pm, but he asked if he could come to see her. The night nurse and a guard greeted him at the door, and they went up to the third floor of the large building. In the day room, the nurse introduced him to Hannah. She was a sweet, silver-haired old-timer with a warm smile and a twinkle in her eyes. He told her about finding the wallet and showed her the letter. The second she saw it, she took a deep breath and said, "this letter was the last contact I ever had with Michael. I loved him very much. But I was only sixteen at the time and mother felt I was too young." "Yes," she continued, "Michael Goldstein was a wonderful person. If you should find him, tell him I think of him often. And ...," she hesitated for a moment, "... I never did marry. I guess no one ever matched up to Michael ..."

When the security guard enquired how his visit to Hannah had been. The man, now on his way out, explained the whole story about how it had really all been about trying to find the owner of a wallet he'd found. He produced the wallet, and when the guard saw it, he immediately said, "Hey, wait a minute! That's Mr. Goldstein's wallet. I'd know it anywhere with that bright red lacing. He's always losing it. I must have found it in the halls at least three times already. He's one of the old-timers on the eighth floor. That's Mike Goldstein's wallet for sure. He probably lost it on one of his walks."

And so a hurried visit was immediately paid to the day room on the eighth floor! The same nurse went over to Mr. Goldstein who put his hand in his back pocket and confirmed his wallet was missing, and that the one being offered to him, was indeed his. The finder of the wallet then admitted that he'd read the letter – explaining he'd done so in the hope of finding out who owned the wallet – and then he added: "Not only did I read it, but I think I know where Hannah is." The old man smiled and asked, "Could you tell me where she is? I was so in love with that girl that when that letter came, my life seemed to end. I never married. I guess I've always loved her."

Soon the elevator was making its way down from the eighth to the third floor. The hallways were darkened but one or two night lights lit the way to the day room, where Hannah was still watching television alone. The nurse walked over to her. "Hannah," she said softly, pointing to Michael, who was waiting in the doorway. "Do you know this man?" She adjusted her glasses, looked for a moment, but didn't say a word. Michael said softly, almost in a whisper, "Hannah, it's Michael. Do you remember me?" She gasped. "Michael! I don't believe it! Michael! It's you! My Michael!" He walked slowly toward her, and they embraced. About three weeks later, they were married - with all the people at the nursing home joining in the celebration. They were given their own room, and a seventy-six-year-old bride and a seventy-nine-year-old groom acted like the two teenagers they'd been when they were forced to part sixty years before. (THE WALLET by Arnold Fine, Readers Digest, 1985).

Think of it. A young man loved his girl so much that he stayed faithful to her and remained single his whole life long because he couldn't love another woman the same way. And a teenage woman remained true to her first love, even as she obeyed her parents' wishes. By contrast, the apostle John wrote to some Christians who'd left their first love (Revelation 2:4). And James wrote to Christians who'd failed to remain faithful to the

Lord, but who had become friends of the world instead (James 4:1-5).

One day long ago, God asked the Old Testament prophet Jeremiah (see Jeremiah 35), to visit a small group of people called the Rechabites, to invite them to the temple, and in a side room there, to offer them wine to drink. Jeremiah makes the arrangements and brings them in. He brings out a tray of glasses filled with wine, just as God had instructed him. But then, most likely, he noticed a sense of discomfort among his guests. 'I'm sorry,' says the leader of the group. 'Didn't you know that we don't drink wine and haven't done so for generations? One of our ancestors, a devout man, commanded us never to drink wine. To this day, we never drink wine.'

Perhaps Jeremiah was then puzzled as to why God had asked him to do this. Then, in effect, God explained: 'I just wanted you to see a living example of how it's possible even for an earthly father to command obedience that lasts for generations. But I've spoken to my people again and again, but they've not obeyed me – they just keep on making excuses for not serving me.'

A human being can be determined enough to follow an earthly leader. By the sheer power of the human will, and by rigid discipline, a man can observe a really tough set of rules. What then does that say about Christians, who – despite the 'regeneration and renewing by the Holy Spirit' (Titus 3:5) – still live unfaithful, disobedient lives?

It's hard to understand how we can compare so unfavourably with unbelievers in this regard. Until, that is, we go back to look again at what James really says in its entirety. He asks:

"What is the source of quarrels and conflicts among you? Is not the source your pleasures that wage war in your members?

You lust and do not have; so you commit murder. You are envious and cannot obtain; so you fight and quarrel. You do not have because you do not ask. You ask and do not receive, because you ask with wrong motives, so that you may spend it on your pleasures. You adulteresses, do you not know that friendship with the world is hostility toward God? Therefore whoever wishes to be a friend of the world makes himself an enemy of God" (James 4:1-4).

It's hard to think of this being the behaviour of believers. But it was. Believers become special targets of the Adversary, and he uses our own lust to bring us down (James 1:14,15). These were believers – here in James chapter 4 – believers whose 'flesh' or sinful nature was out of control. And James goes on to tell them (v.5) that the Bible's always reminding us that our human spirit, as influenced by our fallen (flesh) nature, tends only to envy and lust – and that's what's behind us never being satisfied: with the grass on the other side always seeming to be greener than where we're standing. When we find that happening, it's because our flesh, our fallen, sinful nature, is exerting a greater influence on us than God's Holy Spirit is exerting on us. The remedy is found in the uncompromising words of the Lord Jesus Christ when he said: "If anyone wishes to come after Me, he must deny himself, and take up his cross daily and follow Me" (Luke 9:23).

Notice the uncompromising self-effacing; self-denying; self-sacrificing message of those words - but, yes, a crucifying of the flesh with its passions and desires (Galatians 5:24) is what makes possible our living and walking by the Spirit ... praying also that we may be strengthened with power through his Spirit in our inner being (Ephesians 3:16) to the end that we'll discover that God really "is able to do far more abundantly beyond all that we [currently do] ask or think, according to the power that [already] works within us (Ephesians 3:20).

Let's ask for more of God's power that's already at work within us so that, by living according to the Spirit and not according to the flesh (Romans 8), we'll be able to obey and stay faithful, never leaving our first love.

CHAPTER TWO: SCRIBBLING AND SALIVATING AT THE DOORS OF THE GATE (DAVID)

April 26, 2006, was the day tragedy struck Taylor University in Upland, Indiana in the US. Students and staff were travelling back to campus in a college van when an out of control truck hit them head-on. Four students and a staff member died instantly. Funerals were held and the bereaved families mourned their losses. The VanRyn family received word that their daughter, Laura, though seriously injured and in a coma, had survived the crash – the only student to do so. The entire family rushed to the hospital and kept watch day and night over their daughter. The crash had badly injured and disfigured her.

As the days went by, Laura began to open her eyes and gradually she began to speak. Her family rejoiced at the progress she was making. But then she started to say some really strange things. Her boyfriend felt confused and started asking questions. But they reassured themselves that the strange things she was saying were all due to her head injuries. But when they called her by name she kept shaking her head, and saying her name was not Laura, but Whitney. Oddly enough there had been a Whitney in the van, but she'd been one of those killed outright at the scene of the crash. Her family had already buried her. Why did Laura keep referring to herself as Whitney?

Then, after comparing dental records, officials uncovered a huge blunder. Someone at the scene had wrongly identified the lone student survivor as Laura. In fact, Laura VanRyn was dead.

The young woman in the rehabilitation centre was not Laura, but Whitney Cerak.

Laura's family revealed that they'd suspected that the patient in the hospital was not their daughter for several days before they'd informed officials. Soon after the accident, the Van Ryns had in fact noticed several indications that Whitney was not Laura - such as discovering the difference in Whitney Cerak's teeth and her navel piercing (which Laura Van Ryn did not have), and then of course Whitney Cerak later stated that her name was Whitney, not Laura, after coming out of her coma. Laura's parents revealed that family friends eventually had expressed concerns that the woman they were caring for was not their daughter. The father said Whitney had accused them of being "false parents." Finally, when Whitney told Laura's sister the name of her parents, Newell and Colleen, it was then finally that Laura's parents notified officials of the tragic mistake - more than a month after the accident. They explained their actions by stating that they were convinced by medical personnel that Whitney really was their daughter, but also that emotional distress had kept them from realizing the truth sooner.

The coroner had failed to positively identify all the victims, and soon announced his retirement. The incident made international headlines as a shocking case of mistaken identity between two of the victims. Laura Van Ryn, who died on the scene, was mistaken for the surviving Whitney Cerak. This was due to Whitney Cerak being in a coma for several weeks, a minor resemblance between the two women, swelling to Whitney's face, and the fact that the VanRyn family had been reluctant to personally identify the body. Whitney's (actually Laura's) funeral had been conducted with a closed casket, and the mistake was not discovered until Whitney identified herself after waking up from a coma a month later.

We can only imagine the shifting emotions between the two families involved. One family thought their daughter was dead but found out that she was actually alive; while the other family, having initially rejoiced at the survival of their daughter, later discovered that she'd actually died at the crash scene.

A mistake like this traumatizes, not least because we derive our identity from relationships. Without them, I cannot be me. But, who am I? Before we put our faith in Jesus Christ as our personal Saviour, we were previously identified with Adam, the first human whom God created. We were, as the Bible says, 'in Adam'. Adam, of course, as the Bible's first book reveals, sinned by disobeying God, his creator. He then became the head of a race of sinful human beings to which we all belonged by natural birth. It's as if God viewed us as sinning in and with Adam, the first man.

Unfair, you might think. But only if the story ended there. We thank God, the Bible is the story of two men, the second being Jesus Christ, God's Son sent from heaven. He became also truly human, and was without any personal sin. He offered himself as a sacrifice for our sins when he died on the cross. All those who are joined to him by faith, by a new spiritual birth, are viewed by God as also dying with Christ to the penalty of sin.

The cross of Christ divides between two races of humans: sinners, headed up by Adam; and believers made right with God, and headed up by Christ. This is the only 'racism' that has any validity, because we all belong to the one human race, we are all of one blood. When we come and stand at the cross by faith, God takes us out of Adam and places us in Christ.

This effectively happens at our conversion, but the basis for it was laid at the cross. There, in the purposes of God, we were taken from a position of being 'in Adam' and given a new position of being 'in Christ'. We actually become a different person, with a different identity. New thinking; new ambitions; new standards; a new quality of relationships and of behaviour should flow from that real fact. But do they? Or are people confused as to our true identity? How can a crash victim's mistaken ID be quickly discovered, but we can spend far longer in worldly company without our Christian ID being discovered?

The Apostle Paul gave the answer when he implied how Christians all too easily become 'conformed to the world' (Romans 12:2). What this means is that the outward appearance of our lifestyle looks a lot like that of the non-Christians living around us. What Paul actually said was: "do not be conformed to this world, but be transformed by the renewing of your mind."

So, the remedy's there as well as the problem. Into one of our churches recently walked a Christian believer belonging to a Roma community. He didn't watch TV, wasn't in touch with the news, but knew all the old hymns, and was very enthusiastic about the Bible and his faith. He wasn't conformed to this world at all. His Christian identity was clear. John Bunyan – who wrote the classic, Pilgrim's Progress - also wrote of people like that, he said: "I heard, but ... they were far above, out of my reach. Their talk was about a new birth, the work of God on their hearts ... how God had visited their souls with His love in the Lord Jesus, and with what words and promises they had been refreshed, comforted, and supported against the temptations of the devil ... and methought they spake as if joy did make them speak; they spake with such pleasantness of Scripture language, and with such appearance of grace in all they said, that they were to me as if they had found a new world, as if they were people that dwelt alone, and were not to be reckoned among their neighbours" (John Bunyan in Grace Abounding). By contrast, how long do people need to be in our company before they discover our true identity?

Sure, Bunyan's language there was old-fashioned, and we don't want to appear odd, giving the impression that the Christian message lacks relevance. But if we over-emphasize the value of our street-cred, we lose our message. Christianity isn't meant to be 'cool'. Our Lord taught us to expect that the world will hate us – if it doesn't we're probably not living right. And you know, again we can find an Old Testament example of the same issue: a time when people were unsure whose side David was on, and whether he truly belonged any more among the people of God. In 1 Samuel 21, we read:

"... David arose and fled that day from Saul, and went to Achish king of Gath. But the servants of Achish said to him, "Is this not David the king of the land? Did they not sing of this one as they danced, saying, 'Saul has slain his thousands, And David his ten thousands'?" David took these words to heart and greatly feared Achish king of Gath. So he disguised his sanity before them, and acted insanely in their hands, and scribbled on the doors of the gate, and let his saliva run down into his beard. Then Achish said to his servants, "Behold, you see the man behaving as a madman. Why do you bring him to me? "Do I lack madmen, that you have brought this one to act the madman in my presence? Shall this one come into my house?" (1 Samuel 21:10-15).

David found it convenient to disguise his true identity by acting the part of the madman. Whenever we feel intimidated by the worldly company we're in, we can act like we're one of them – but surely that's madness on our part too? Let's come back to the sober-mindedness of Romans 12:2 – "And ... not be conformed to this world, but be transformed by the renewing of your mind." The transforming mentioned is like the word for

Christ's own transfiguration: it's a change that comes from within: one which reveals our true identity. This is so different from the type of conforming that's typical of the Devil: which is an outer change that conceals the true identity within. I'll leave you with the question: is your true identity clear?

CHAPTER THREE: A VINEYARD IN JEZREEL (NABOTH)

Once in an in-flight magazine there was a feature on ethics. It began with a provocative story which – without doubt - was designed to get the reader's attention – and probably usually succeeded.

The writer described a man on board an airplane who propositioned the woman sitting next to him for one million dollars. In other words, he asked this stranger if she would be prepared to sleep with him if he paid her a million dollars. The woman was scandalized that this total stranger would dare to offer her a million dollars if she slept with him. But she pursued the conversation and gradually began to entertain the possibility of how she could so easily become a millionaire.

It wasn't too long before they set the time, the terms, and the conditions. Then, just before they were to leave the airplane, the man confessed and said: 'I have to admit that I'd don't really have a million dollars – would just 10 dollars be OK?' On the verge of smacking him across the face for such an insult, the woman snapped back, 'What do you think I am?' 'That's already been established,' he replied. 'Now we're just haggling over the price.' Mmm ... do our principles also have a price limit?

James Patterson and Peter Kim wrote a book entitled The Day America Told the Truth. In it they asked the question, "What are you willing to do for $10,000,000?" They polled a number of Americans to see if they would agree to any of the following in return for receiving $10,000,000. Here's what they found:

25% would abandon their entire family for 10 million dollars.

25% would abandon their church for 10 million dollars.

23% would become prostitutes for a week or more in exchange for 10 million dollars.

16% would leave their spouses for 10 million dollars.

10% would withhold testimony and let a murderer go free for 10 million dollars.

7% would murder a stranger for 10 million dollars.

3% would put their children up for adoption for 10 million dollars.

Can you believe that? Two-thirds of all Americans polled would agree to at least one of the conditions for $10,000,000. What'd you be willing to do for $10,000,000? Hopefully, you'd be among the one-third who'd refuse to sell their integrity! There's a man whom we meet in the Bible who definitely would come into that category. His name is Naboth, and his story is found in 1 Kings 21.

"Now it came about after these things that Naboth the Jezreelite had a vineyard which was in Jezreel beside the palace of Ahab king of Samaria. Ahab spoke to Naboth, saying, "Give me your vineyard, that I may have it for a vegetable garden because it is close beside my house, and I will give you a better vineyard than

it in its place; if you like, I will give you the price of it in money."
But Naboth said to Ahab, "The LORD forbid me that I should
give you the inheritance of my fathers."

So Ahab came into his house sullen and vexed because of the
word which Naboth the Jezreelite had spoken to him; for he said,
"I will not give you the inheritance of my fathers." And he lay
down on his bed and turned away his face and ate no food. But
Jezebel his wife came to him and said to him, "How is it that your
spirit is so sullen that you are not eating food?" So he said to her,
"Because I spoke to Naboth the Jezreelite and said to him, 'Give
me your vineyard for money; or else, if it pleases you, I will give
you a vineyard in its place.' But he said, 'I will not give you my
vineyard'" (1 Kings 21:16).

It was a case of no sale at any price for Naboth. The point
we're making is not about sentiment; it's about principle. How
can people like Naboth refuse to compromise at any price, and
yet we're sometimes prepared to sell the truth? I ask you: 'What
price your convictions?' Some people's career takes over their
lives, and success is like an addiction. Peer pressure puts us under
tremendous strain to sell out and compromise Christian
standards.

A similar old story out of India has a different twist to
Naboth's. It tells of a wealthy man who came into a small village
to buy it. Hut by hut, shack by shack, he bought every square
inch of the village, except for what belonged to one old man, who
refused to sell his hut in the centre of the village to this man who
wanted to boast that he owned the whole village. The rich man
doubled his offer not once, but twice, but still the old man
refused to sell, saying he'd not sell at any price. The rich man
tried to find something the old man would take in exchange for
his old hut, but every effort failed. The rest of the village
belonged to the rich man, but he couldn't own the old man's hut

however he tried. Whenever the greedy landowner was showing off his estate to his friends, as they passed through the centre of the village, the old man who had refused to sell out to him, would step out from his doorway and say to the village-owner's guests: 'Don't let him tell you he owns it all, he doesn't own this part of it! This hut right in the middle belongs to me!'

Looking at our life from another angle: you may know the Saviour, and you may have been baptized, be a regular at the church services, teaching a Sunday school class etc., but when you worship God you still hear the taunt of our enemy the Devil saying to you 'don't forget, there's a bit of you that still belongs to me!' It's sad if our Christian principles have a selling price; and it's also tragic if we won't turn from worldly behaviour for any price!

The Roman persecution of Christians began during the reign of Nero and persisted until Christianity was recognized as a legitimate religion by the Emperor Constantine some 250 years later. Christians were denounced as enemies of men and the gods and therefore subject to the severest tortures. Conviction didn't lead inevitably to execution. Pardon would be granted if the Christian threw a few grains of incense on the altar of the pagan god. If this offer was refused, more severe measures such as scourging or other tortures were implemented. If these failed, the victim was led to the circus or amphitheatre and subjected to a horrible death for the amusement of the crowd.

Perpetua was a young woman of noble birth. She was twenty-two, a wife, a mother of a young son and a Christian. In the city of Carthage in North Africa on March 7 of the year A.D. 203 she was put to death for her religious convictions. Her story comes to us from three eyewitness accounts written shortly after her death. Perpetua was one of five Christians condemned to death in the arena. Perpetua's father was a pagan and often came to the prison (many times with her son in his arms) – he came to plead with his daughter to renounce her religion and save her life – but all to no avail. It appears that we have on record a transcript of a conversation she had with her father while she waited for her death.

"When I was in the hands of the persecutors, my father in his tender solicitude tried hard to pervert me from the faith. 'My father,' I said, 'you see this pitcher. Can we call it by any other name than what it is?' 'No,' he said. 'Nor can I call myself by any other name than that of Christian.' 'Daughter,' he said, 'have pity on my gray hairs ... Do not give me over to disgrace. Behold [your] brothers, [your] mother, and [your] aunt: behold [your]child who cannot live without [you]. Do not destroy us all.' My father, kiss[ed] my hands, and thr[ew] himself at my feet. And I wept because of my father, for he alone of all my family would not rejoice in my martyrdom. So I comforted him, saying: 'In this trial what God determines will take place. We are not in our own keeping, but in God's.' So he left me - weeping bitterly."

On March 7, Perpetua and her four companions were led to the arena where the crowd demanded they should be scourged. Then a boar, a bear and a leopard were set loose on the men; while the women were attacked by a wild bull. Wounded, Perpetua was then put to the sword. She didn't sell out. She held fast to her convictions, and became an inspiring example of integrity.

When king David's son, Absalom rebelled against him, David commanded his generals to spare his son's life in the inevitable battle. Absalom's forces were defeated, and Absalom himself fled, but soon found himself trapped. One soldier loyal to David saw him and reported his whereabouts to one of the generals, a man called Joab.

"Then Joab said to the man who had told him, "Now behold, you saw him! Why then did you not strike him there to the ground? And I would have given you ten pieces of silver and a belt." The man said to Joab, "Even if I should receive a thousand pieces of silver in my hand, I would not put out my hand against the king's son; for in our hearing the king charged you and Abishai and Ittai, saying, 'Protect for me the young man Absalom!'" (2 Samuel 18:12).

Not for ten nor even a thousand pieces of silver would that man have disobeyed his king's command. What about us? I'm privileged to know some Christians who have passed this test magnificently. But, what about us? Would we dare to disobey one of our Lord's commands if someone offered us $10 million?

CHAPTER FOUR: A LOVE THAT'S REAL

I remember hearing about a time when a room full of people was asked what the most important question was. Finally, one man thoughtfully replied: 'The most important thing to know is the answer to the question: "Am I loved?" He explained his thinking like this: he said if the answer was 'no,' then none of life's accomplishments really mattered; but if the answer was yes – meaning we knew we were loved – then we could endure great ordeals and hardships. There's a lot of truth in that. We've been designed with a capacity to give and receive love: to be in a web of supportive relationships. It's when a man's progress at the office comes at the expense of his family life that he discovers – often sadly too late – that relationships matter more than achievements.

On that tragic day, the 11th of September, 2001, there are many records of the last phone transmissions from people in the doomed twin towers or from those captive in the planes that were being flown as lethal weapons into those towers in that sickening act of terrorism. None of these final messages enquired about the size of one's bank balance or if promotion was imminent. Three words spoken in every message were: 'I love you.'

As I travel around, I often get asked the question: 'Why did God allow sin to enter his perfect creation? My answer invariably is that God could certainly have avoided it had he so chosen. He could have created an assembly line of beings who were incapable of making wrong moral choices: a robotic race that could do nothing but love him. And so they'd love God for ever, simply because they'd no other choice but to do so. But how meaningful is that? The man who spoke earlier about knowing we're loved as the most important thing wasn't thinking about a forced kind of love. Love is all about choices. People need to know the love they experience is real – as the following story shows.

Six minutes to six, said the great round clock over the information booth in Grand Central Station. The tall young Army lieutenant, who'd just come from the direction of the tracks, lifted his sunburned face, and narrowed his eyes to note the exact time. His heart was pounding with a beat that shocked him because he couldn't control it. In six minutes, he would see the woman who'd filled such a special place in his life for the past 13 months, the woman he'd never seen, yet whose written words had sustained him.

Five minutes to six. He placed himself as close as he could to the information booth. Lieutenant Blandford remembered one night in particular, in the worst of the fighting, when his plane had been caught in the midst of a pack of enemy aircraft. He'd even seen the grinning face of one of the enemy pilots. In one of his letters, he'd confessed to the woman he was now waiting to meet that he often felt fear, and only a few days before this battle, he'd received her answer: "Of course you fear ... all brave men do. Didn't King David know fear? That's why he wrote the 23rd Psalm. Next time you doubt yourself, I want you to hear my voice reciting to you: 'Yea, though I walk through the valley of the shadow of death, I shall fear no evil, for Thou art with me.'" And he'd remembered; he'd heard her imagined voice, and it'd renewed his strength and skill. Now he was going to hear her real voice.

Four minutes to six. His face grew sharp. Under the immense, starred roof, people were walking fast, like threads of colour being woven into a gray web. A girl passed close to him, and

Lieutenant Blandford reacted. She was wearing a red flower in her suit lapel, but it was a crimson sweet pea, not the little red rose they had agreed upon as a means of identification. Besides, this girl was too young, about 18, whereas Hollis Meynell had frankly told him she was 30. "Well, what of it?" he had answered. "I'm 32." He was really only 29.

Three minutes to six. His mind went back to that book – that one book out of the hundreds of Army library books sent to the Florida training camp. 'Of Human Bondage', it was; and throughout the book were notes in a woman's writing. He'd always hated that writing-in-habit, but these remarks were different. He'd never believed that a woman could see into a man's heart so tenderly, so understandingly. Her name was on the bookplate: Hollis Meynell. He'd got hold of a New York City telephone book and found her address. He'd written, she'd answered. Next day he'd been shipped out, but they'd gone on writing.

Two minutes to six. For 13 months, she'd faithfully replied, and more than replied. When his letters didn't arrive she wrote anyway, and now he believed he loved her, and she loved him. But she'd refused all his pleas to send him her photograph. She'd explained: "If your feeling for me has any reality, any honest basis, what I look like won't matter. Suppose I'm beautiful. I'd always be haunted by the feeling that you had been taking a chance on just that, and that kind of love would disgust me. Suppose I'm plain (and you must admit that this is more likely). Then I'd always fear that you were going on writing to me only because you were lonely and had no one else. No, don't ask for my picture. When you come to New York, you'll see me and then you'll make your decision. Remember, both of us are free to stop or to go on after that - whichever we choose ..."

One minute to six - Lieutenant Blandford's heart leaped higher than his plane had ever done. A young woman was coming toward him. Her figure was long and slim; her blond hair lay back in curls from delicate ears. Her eyes were blue as flowers, in her pale green suit, she was like springtime come alive. He moved toward her, entirely forgetting to notice that she was wearing no rose, and as he moved, a small, provocative smile curved her lips. "Going my way, soldier?" she murmured. Uncontrollably, he made one step closer to her. Then he saw Hollis Meynell.

She was standing almost directly behind the girl, a woman well past 40, her graying hair tucked under a worn hat. She was more than plump; her thick-ankled feet were thrust into low-heeled shoes. But she wore a red rose in the rumpled lapel of her brown coat. The girl in the green suit was walking quickly away. Blandford felt as though he were being split in two, so keen was his desire to follow the girl, yet so deep was his longing for the woman whose spirit had truly companioned and upheld his own; and there she stood.

Her pale, plump face was gentle and sensible; he could see that now. Her gray eyes had a warm, kindly twinkle. Lieutenant Blandford did not hesitate. His fingers gripped the small worn, blue leather copy of 'Of Human Bondage', which was to identify him to her. This wouldn't be love, but it'd be something precious, something perhaps even rarer than love - a friendship for which he'd been and must ever be grateful. He squared his broad shoulders, saluted and held the book out toward the woman, although even while he spoke he felt shocked by the bitterness of his disappointment. "I'm Lieutenant John Blandford, and you - you are Miss Meynell. I'm so glad you could meet me. May ... may I take you to dinner?" The woman's face broadened in a tolerant smile. "I don't know what this is all about, son," she answered. "That young lady in the green suit -

the one who just went by - begged me to wear this rose on my coat. And she said that if you asked me to go out with you, I should tell you that she's waiting for you in that big restaurant across the street. She said it was some kind of a test. I've got two boys serving with the US armed forces myself, so I didn't mind to oblige you."

God's love for us is real, God's actions at the cross prove that. But what about our love for him in response? Even as Christians, our love for the Lord might not even match the calibre of John Blandford's love for Miss Meynell. And it matters to the Lord. Three times he probes the depth and sincerity of the love of his followers in the space of a few verses in John 14: "If you love Me, you will keep My commandments." The old hymn says 'trust and obey for it's the only way ...' It's the sure way of showing our love for the Lord. If we don't live true to the Word of God, then the love we profess for the Lord is suspect. And this is a theme the Lord returns to again in verse 21 when he says ... "He who has My commandments and keeps them is the one who loves Me; and he who loves Me will be loved by My Father, and I will love him and will disclose Myself to him."

The rewards of loving the Lord are mentioned. They are (1) to be loved by the Father in a special way and (2) to receive an enhanced disclosure of the Lord himself. In John 16:27, the Lord again says: "the Father Himself loves you, because you have loved Me." So often here the Father's love for us is bound to our love for the Lord. For the third time in the space of a few verses in John 14, the Lord speaks like this when he says in verse 23: "If anyone loves Me, he will keep My word; and My Father will love him, and We will come to him and make Our abode with him.

Again, love for the Lord is evidenced by obeying the Word, the things we find in the Bible. Far from despising faithfully following God's Word in all that it plainly teaches us – as if it was some technical thing rather than anything spiritual - this is, in fact, the plainest revealed way of showing true heart devotion to Christ. Perhaps the Lord's challenge to us today is the same simple but profound challenge which he put three times to Peter: when he asked: 'Do you love me? Do you truly love me?' When we choose to obey, and to live biblically, we prove that our love for the Lord is real – and that matters to him – it matters to him very much indeed as the repeated emphasis of John chapter 14 shows.

CHAPTER FIVE: THE PROCEEDS OF A PROPERTY DEAL (ANANIAS AND SAPPHIRA)

Bobby Jones (1902-1971) was a lawyer and amateur golfer. He was also the first to achieve the Grand Slam – meaning he won the four major tournaments in a single year. From 1923 through 1930 he won 13 championships in those four annual tournaments – a record, in fact, that was to remain unequalled until Jack Nicklaus broke it in 1973.

But while this clearly proves his golfing skills; it doesn't tell us much at all about the man. There was something even more impressive than his golfing skills – and that something was his integrity. This was once demonstrated in a national championship. Bobby Jones drove his ball into the woods, and when preparing to play the ball, accidentally nudged it. Although no one saw him move the ball, he penalized himself one stroke, which caused him to lose the game by that same slenderest of margins – by a single stroke. When someone later got to hear about what had happened and praised him for his integrity, he was quite dismissive about it and said, "You might as well praise a man for not robbing a bank."

That's a very revealing answer. It was as clear-cut as that in his mind. Right was right; and wrong was wrong – no matter what. The scale of the wrong made no difference; nor did it matter whether or not anyone was watching. Integrity is about living by our principles – even when no-one else is watching. It's about doing what is right rather than what we can get away with.

But the question I want us to think about today is this: How can others outside of any known intimacy with Christ exhibit such impressive integrity while we struggle? Like us, some of the earliest Christians struggled with the issue. The end of Acts chapter 4 and beginning of chapter 5 opens a window for us into what was going on in the first local church of God in Jerusalem:

"... there was not a needy person among them, for all who were owners of land or houses would sell them and bring the proceeds of the sales and lay them at the apostles' feet, and they would be distributed to each as any had need. Now Joseph, a Levite of Cyprian birth, who was also called Barnabas by the apostles (which translated means Son of Encouragement), and who owned a tract of land, sold it and brought the money and laid it at the apostles' feet. But a man named Ananias, with his wife Sapphira, sold a piece of property, and kept back some of the price for himself, with his wife's full knowledge, and bringing a portion of it, he laid it at the apostles' feet. But Peter said, "Ananias, why has Satan filled your heart to lie to the Holy Spirit and to keep back some of the price of the land? While it remained unsold, did it not remain your own? And after it was sold, was it not under your control? Why is it that you have conceived this deed in your heart? You have not lied to men but to God."

And as he heard these words, Ananias fell down and breathed his last; and great fear came over all who heard of it. The young men got up and covered him up, and after carrying him out, they buried him. Now there elapsed an interval of about three hours, and his wife came in, not knowing what had happened. And Peter responded to her, "Tell me whether you sold the land for such and such a price?" And she said, "Yes, that was the price." Then Peter said to her, "Why is it that you have agreed together to put the Spirit of the Lord to the test? Behold, the feet of those who have buried your husband are at the door, and they will carry you out as well." And immediately she fell at his feet and breathed her last, and the young men came in and found her dead, and they carried her out and buried her beside her husband. And great fear came over the whole church, and over all who heard of these things" (Acts 4:34-5:10).

Ananias and Sapphira were not the persons they pretended to be. We only have integrity when we're the good person we appear to be. It's the opposite of hypocrisy. As Socrates (469 - 399 BC) said, "The greatest way to live with honour in this world is to be what we pretend to be." So integrity is about not projecting a better image of ourselves than is deserved – which is what Ananias and Sapphira were doing. Integrity, as we've illustrated already, is when the thoughts of our heart are consistent in every way with the actions of our hands or the words of our lips. Psalm 17 is a psalm of David, and this is what he said:

"Hear a just cause, O LORD, give heed to my cry; Give ear to my prayer, which is not from deceitful lips ... Let my judgment [or decision] come forth from Your presence ... You have tried my heart; You have visited me by night; You have tested me and You find nothing; I have purposed that my mouth will not transgress... by the word of Your lips I have kept from the paths of the violent. My steps have held fast to Your paths. My feet have not slipped ..." (Psalm 17:1-5).

Here, David is conscious of his own integrity before God while surrounded by enemies. He's asking God to hear his righteous cause, to hear to his prayer. This is the honest prayer of a genuinely righteous man, and so its effectiveness is guaranteed. A life of integrity before God doesn't just materialize all by itself. David had resolved not to sin, and was determined to keep himself separate from the ways of the world, the ways of those who destroy. His life, he says, had been modelled on God's

Word. And because David's words here are found among God's inspired writings, we can be totally sure this is an accurate assessment of himself and not just empty boasting or him simply being generous with himself.

I came across a modern example of that when I discovered an article commemorating the birthday of evangelist Billy Graham. Religious News Service writer, Randall Balmer, wrote of Graham's integrity saying that in Graham's lifetime there've been many other evangelists who have fallen because of various moral indiscretions. But throughout a long career there'd never been a serious charge of financial, sexual, or any other kind of wrongdoing levelled against Graham. By all accounts this was a state of affairs that was not simply left to materialize by itself. Early in his career, Graham gathered his associates into a hotel room to discuss how they might avoid some of the pitfalls that had, sadly, claimed the reputation of other evangelists. Graham resolved never to exaggerate attendance figures at their meetings, to accept only fixed salaries, and set up elaborate precautions to protect themselves from sexual temptation or even the appearance of anything improper. The writer then suggested that in an age that has seen evangelists fall in all manner of spectacular scandals, Graham's greatest legacy may be his integrity.

As that illustrates, integrity really does take conscious – even planned - effort. In another of his psalms, Psalm 101:2-4, David says: "I will give heed to the blameless way. When will You come to me? I will walk within my house in the integrity of my heart. I will set no worthless thing before my eyes; I hate the work of those who fall away; It shall not fasten its grip on me. A perverse heart shall depart from me; I will know no evil."

Like Bobby Jones, with whose story we opened the chapter, the man who did not cheat in the smallest degree when no one was looking, so David says that within his house, when no-one else was looking, he was determined to tolerate no evil in his heart. With an act of his will, he says 'I will set no worthless thing before my eyes ... I will know no evil.' In these days when the internet brings the whole world – including potentially a whole world of evil - into our homes and into the privacy of our bedrooms, these words are really worth emphasizing again: 'I will set no worthless thing before my eyes.' What we do when we're alone is the testing ground of our integrity.

David says there, in that psalm, that he hates the work of those who fall away. How interesting here that the work of those who fall away, the work of apostasy, is shown to have as its source, its root, the loss of integrity. Failure in the Christian life is like a slow puncture. Falling away doesn't happen suddenly. It begins some time before with a loss of integrity. More positively, as we plan to maintain our integrity – for example by setting no worthless thing before our eyes – we're actually planning to avoid the work of apostasy, or falling away. With sheer determination David says "it shall not fasten its grip on me." David was known in the Bible for the integrity of his heart (Psalm 78:72) – which is shown here to be the opposite of a perverse heart. Our response to the Bible is not only to be intellectual and emotional, but volitional as well. We are to imitate David when he says: "I will know no evil."

CHAPTER SIX: THE SNARE OF THE DEVIL

In 1974, a rich heiress by the name of Patty Hearst was kidnapped by a radical group known as the Symbionese Liberation Army (SLA). There were several negotiation attempts for her release but they all failed. Then it seemed like the next we knew was she was assisting her captors two months later in a bank robbery! She was arrested, and put on trial. During her trial her defence was that she'd been suffering from what was called Stockholm Syndrome – a condition in which victims become so dependent on their captors that they even become sympathetic to them. Her defence failed however, and Hearst was convicted and sentenced to prison.

We're so easily persuaded by our captor to do his will. Our would-be captor is the Devil (if we allow him). He oppresses us and tries to devour us. But too often we don't even resist, but willingly take part in his evil schemes! It's like a spiritual Stockholm syndrome. When I was reminded of Patty Hearst, I got to thinking about 2 Timothy 2 where Paul says to Timothy:

"Now flee from youthful lusts and pursue righteousness, faith, love and peace, with those who call on the Lord from a pure heart. But refuse foolish and ignorant speculations, knowing that they produce quarrels. The Lord's bond-servant must not be quarrelsome, but be kind to all, able to teach, patient when wronged, with gentleness correcting those who are in opposition, if perhaps God may grant them repentance leading to the knowledge of the truth, and they may come to their senses and escape from the snare of the devil, having been held captive by him to do his will" (2 Timothy 2:22-26).

See what I mean about the Devil taking us captive, and then – all too readily, it seems – we fulfil his agenda, not the Lord's. We can shake our head in disbelief about the actions of someone like Patty Hearst who sided with her captors, but we often fail to see that we do the same. The Devil takes us captive, and we end up doing his will!

The instructions we've read were the apostle Paul's instructions to Timothy if he was going to be a true servant of Jesus Christ - or as it's put here: the Lord's bond-servant. The role of being the Lord's bond-servant is open to any one of us – anyone who puts doing the Lord's will at the forefront of his or her life. In order to do that, there are things we must run away from. Paul describes them as youthful lusts and avoiding being quarrelsome. And if these are things to run away from, there're also things we're to run after – like righteousness, faith, love and peace while worshipping with a pure heart. Then there's the kindness, gentleness and patience which is especially necessary when teaching others to know the will of God more carefully – and all the time side-stepping time-wasting debates.

These things can be said in a few words, but living up to them is challenging, isn't it? It's tough even to know sometimes when it's worth continuing a debate. Defending our faith is one thing – and we've got to be prepared to do it. But many engage in debate with us who are not true searchers after truth. They love the sport of debate but they don't love the truth. In a mountain village in the Far East I recently met a man like that. He denied Jesus was more than a man. He kept trying to make a big deal out of the fact that the Bible doesn't record Jesus as saying directly 'I am God.' After pointing out he was making God a liar by disbelieving the Bible's clear testimony in verses like Titus 2:13 where Jesus is described as 'our great God and Saviour,' I had to leave him with the challenge of whether he'd ever in his life said: 'I am human.'

The fact he hadn't didn't disprove his obvious humanity, of course. But then we have to turn from such as refuse to love the truth, for to continue to answer them simply gives them multiplied reasons for misinterpretation. The servant of the Lord will always experience opposition. It stems from our Adversary the Devil who also tries to directly trap or ensnare us in his schemes. We have to confess he's quite successful. He knows as long as we stay close to God he's no power over us, so he tries to:

1) Keep us busy with non-essentials.

2) Tempt us to overspend and go into debt.

3) Make us work long hours to maintain empty lifestyles.

4) Discourage us from spending family time, for when homes disintegrate there's no refuge from work.

5) Overstimulate our minds with television and computers so that we can't hear God speaking to us.

6) Fill our coffee tables with newspapers and magazines so we've no time for Bible reading.

7) Flood our mail boxes with promotions and get-rich-quick schemes; to keep us chasing material things.

8) Put glamorous models on TV and on magazine covers to keep us focused on outward appearances; that way we'll be dissatisfied with ourselves and our partners.

9) Make sure married couples are too exhausted for physical intimacy; that way we'll be tempted to look elsewhere.

10) Make us over-committed to 'good' causes to the extent we don't have any time for 'eternal' ones.

11) Make us self-sufficient. Keep us so busy working in our own strength that we'll never know the joy of God's power working through us. (W4T 2/12/10)

In any one of these ways, we can be co-opted by the Devil to do his will. He did it with Peter and he did it with Ananias and Sapphira. With Peter, the Devil got him to concentrate on human, worldly matters. With Ananias and Sapphira, it was a case of exploiting their greed and desire to be seen to be more spiritual than they really were. We can all too easily fall into the same traps. As our captor, the Devil easily persuades us to do his will. Too often we don't even resist, but willingly take part in his evil schemes! As we said when we reviewed the story of Patty Hearst, it's like a spiritual Stockholm syndrome – where, if we recall – Stockholm syndrome is the term given to the psychological phenomenon when people who've been taken hostage end up switching sides. Bob Dylan once sang a song: 'You gotta serve somebody' and he was right. The Apostle Paul puts it like this in Romans chapter 6:

"Therefore do not let sin reign in your mortal body so that you obey its lusts, and do not go on presenting the members of your body to sin as instruments of unrighteousness; but present yourselves to God as those alive from the dead, and your members as instruments of righteousness to God. For sin shall not be master over you, for you are not under law but under grace. What then? Shall we sin because we are not under law but under grace? May it never be! Do you not know that when you present yourselves to someone as slaves for obedience, you are slaves of the one whom you obey, either of sin resulting in death, or of obedience resulting in righteousness? But thanks be to God that though you were slaves of sin, you became obedient from the heart to that form of teaching to which you were committed, and having been freed from sin, you became slaves of righteousness" (Romans 6:12-18).

Before we came to know Christ, we were slaves to sin. As Jesus said (John 8:34), anyone who commits sin is a slave to sin. Even after we're saved, we still sin. In fact, the Apostle John tells us that to say otherwise is to make God a liar (1 John 1:10). There's no sinless perfection this side of heaven. But, by relying on the power of God's indwelling Spirit, there's no longer any reason for sin to dominate our lives as it once did before we came to know Christ. Under the Law, people couldn't gain the mastery over sin in their lives, but we're not under Law, but under grace. This makes a vital practical difference. By the grace of God we can present ourselves to God for his service. We can use our minds and hands to do his will and to advance his purposes in our lives.

For sure, we've got to serve somebody. It's a stark choice. Either we're obedient slaves to sinful practices or obedient slaves to righteous living. As baptized followers of Christ – which is the whole context of Romans chapter 6 – it's clear that we should be committed to doing what's right at every opportunity. Paul talks here (in v.17) about the form or pattern of teaching. This, of course, is what's known biblically as the Apostles' teaching, which Paul and the other apostles taught as from the Lord himself. The idea here is that this body of Christian doctrine acts like a mould to shape our lives in service for the Lord Jesus.

It's not just information for our heads: it's presented here as the way of righteousness (see 2 Peter 2:21). It's precisely obedience to the pattern of biblical teaching set out by the apostles of Christ which defines righteous living. When you pour water in a glass and freeze it, the now frozen water takes the shape of the glass. Just as the water was presented to the glass, we're presented to the pattern of New Testament teaching so that our lives are truly shaped by it to do what's right.

CHAPTER SEVEN: TEN SILVER COINS AND A SUIT (THE YOUNG LEVITE)

The young man walked the winding path up the hill. He was heading into the hill country, known then as the hill country of Ephraim. This was a new venture for him, belonging as he did down in the town of Bethlehem, the city of David. But as he walked away he felt an exhilarating surge of freedom. The responsibilities of the service he'd been reared to perform with all its biblical rituals now lay behind him.

He'd no particular destination in mind as he walked along. He was ready to explore whatever might come along. There was a real sense of excitement in not being able to predict what lay in store. The mood of these days was one of 'doing your own thing.' And that's what he fully intended to do. It'd be good to break with tradition, and to really 'find himself.'

As it turned out, he didn't have to search long for an opportunity. An interesting challenge – one that seemed ideally suited to him - presented itself to him quite early on. In one place where he found lodgings, his host enquired after his background, likely his accent gave him away as not being local. He began explaining that he was a Levite, belonging to that tribe of Israel which had by God's initiative been given the task, even the privilege, of assisting the priests in their duties around God's house. That should've been enough for any man, but somehow he'd grown weary of it. What was it that had bred discontent in this young man? Was it the restless spirit of youth? A sense of needing to move with the times perhaps – did the careful instructions and provisions of the Law of Moses seem a bit outdated to him, I wonder? Had he inherited an adventurous spirit from his parents? It seems his father had married outside the tribe of Levi - married a woman of Judah, in fact, and so they weren't living in any one of the Levitical cities. Did this young man want to distance himself one stage further from living strictly as a Levite? Or was he simply making the same mistake each rising generation tends to make: by thinking there's greater freedom in exercising a choice that strays from God's prescribed path.

That reminds me of a professor who once asked his class which of three persons had the greatest freedom. Was it the person who was incapable of not sinning (hardly likely since that person would be a slave to sin); or was it the person capable of both sinning and not sinning; or was it simply the person who was incapable of sinning? As indicated, the students quickly rule out the first chap, because he was a slave to sin. With a little thought, it was then suggested that the person capable of both sinning and not sinning seemed to have the most freedom. But a little more thought caused some to see a difficulty with that. After all, God is not capable of sinning, and surely no-one has more freedom than God, so it's got to be the third chap – the one incapable of sinning.

But this Levite thought greater freedom might be found in a path of his own choosing and preference rather than God's. The Levite was, of course, capable of sinning, and that's what he was doing, deluding himself that this was what it meant to be truly free. Once this young man had explained about his Levitical background, an idea suddenly flashed into the mind of his host. He, too, had kicked against God's laws, even the ten commandments. For one thing, he'd broken the command against stealing. At one point he'd even stolen a large sum of money in silver from his own mother, but then his conscience had finally got the better of him and he'd returned it. With foolish indulgence, his mother had allowed him to use some of it to make household idols – and so it was that another of God's commands had come to be broken. Not only idols had been made, but also a graven and a molten image along with a shrine and an ephod. At this time one of his own sons was acting as the family priest. This was all far removed from what the young Levite knew well was God's way.

But suddenly the young traveller realized he was being offered a job by his host whom, by now, he'd discovered was called Micah. Would he like to lodge here permanently and take over from Micah's son? From Micah's point of view, it seemed desirable to secure the services of a trained, professional priestly assistant. So desirable in fact, that he'd make it worth the young man's while. Not only would he receive daily provisions, but there was a salary on offer which extended to 10 pieces of silver annually with a new suit of clothes each year thrown in.

That seemed good to the young man, and he accepted the deal. Not only would this be a new challenge, a refreshing change, it'd allow him to experiment with different religious ideas, ones which weren't constrained by strict biblical requirements. He'd gain independence, free from having to comply with others. Besides that, there was the attraction of new financial security, not to mention a certain status – after all there weren't likely to be other Levites around there. And so, doubtless with some considerations like those, the compromise was readily reached. The young Levite seemed to justify the move easily, despite it being shockingly different from his Bible-based background.

This story, which closely follows the narrative of Judges chapter 17, stands as a warning from a bygone age of how easy it is in any generation to rationalize a departure from biblical teaching. The young Levite whose adventure we've been following sold out his principles big-time for 10 pieces of silver and a new suit of clothes. We rush to criticize him, but how different are we?

We've mentioned before, but will do again here, of how James Patterson and Peter Kim once wrote a book entitled The Day America Told the Truth. In their book they asked the question, "What are you willing to do for $10,000,000?" They polled a number of Americans to see if they would agree to any of the following in return for receiving $10,000,000. Here is what they found:

25% would abandon their entire family for 10 million dollars.

25% would abandon their church for 10 million dollars.

23% would become prostitutes for a week or more in exchange for 10 million dollars.

16% would give up their American citizenship for 10 million dollars.

16% would leave their spouses for 10 million dollars.

10% would withhold testimony and let a murderer go free for 10 million dollars.

7% would murder a stranger for 10 million dollars.

3% would put their children up for adoption for 10 million dollars.

Two-thirds of all Americans polled would agree to at least one of the conditions for $10,000,000. What would you be willing to do for $10,000,000? Hopefully, you would be among the one-third who would refuse to sell their integrity.

The Bible proverb gives us timeless wisdom when it counsels us to 'buy truth, and do not sell it' (Proverbs 23:23). An inspiring biblical example which contrasts sharply with the young Levite is found in 2 Samuel chapter 18 which describes the sequel and showdown to the rebellion which David's son, Absalom, staged against him. Of course, David wanted the rebellion crushed, but not at the expense of the life of his rebellious son. He gave instruction that Absalom was not to be killed. This is what happened next:

"Now Absalom happened to meet the servants of David. For Absalom was riding on his mule, and the mule went under the thick branches of a great oak. And his head caught fast in the oak, so he was left hanging between heaven and earth, while the mule that was under him kept going. When a certain man saw it, he told Joab and said, "Behold, I saw Absalom hanging in an oak." Then Joab said to the man who had told him, "Now behold, you saw him! Why then did you not strike him there to the ground? And I would have given you ten pieces of silver and a belt." The man said to Joab, "Even if I should receive a thousand pieces of silver in my hand, I would not put out my hand against the king's son; for in our hearing the king charged you and Abishai and Ittai, saying, 'Protect for me the young man Absalom!'" (2 Samuel 18:9-12).

Here was a man who could not be induced to defy his king's command – even for a very significant amount of money. Our Lord and our King, who is king David's greater son, has given us his commandments through the writing of his apostles in the pages of the New Testament. We, too, like the young man, we began considering, might be tempted to experiment, to try something new, more up-to-date, more 'with-it', more seemingly rewarding and successful. It may not be financial inducement, or anything we'd recognize as status-seeking, that draws us to compromise previously held convictions, but perhaps we're only rationalizing some kind of motivation that's worth little more than 10 silver coins and a new suit. Don't sell the truth at any price, is the Bible's clear warning. The soldier loved his king and respected his commands, will we not do the same? Jesus says: "If you love Me, you will keep My commandments" (John 14:15).

CHAPTER EIGHT: TWO MULES' LOAD OF EARTH (NAAMAN)

The man was a decorated warrior, victorious in many campaigns, and respected by the king. He was a military man at the very top of his career, but there was one battle he was losing – and that was his personal fight against the dread disease of leprosy. Naaman's home, for that was the name of this army captain, contained the spoils of war from different conquests, but one was to become of special value to him. She was a young girl taken captive from the land of Israel, from among God's people, and she now served his wife.

It appears that she was a helpful girl with a pleasing disposition. When you consider she'd been uprooted from her family at an early age and removed to a foreign land, this is all the more remarkable. She held no bitterness or resentment, it seemed, against those who were now her owners, and from that fact, perhaps, we can assume they treated her well.

Naaman's disease couldn't be hidden. It was the only thing that troubled that otherwise successful home. It didn't go unnoticed even by the young captive slave who bore no ill will against her captor. One day, when a suitable opportunity came, she dared to say to her mistress that she wished that her master, the army captain, could visit the prophet who lived back in her native land. Before her captivity, she'd been aware of his reputation and possibly even had known of some of his exploits directly. She certainly knew the power of God was with him, and often with miraculous results. In her youthful earnest way, she testified of all this to the captain's wife. When she said: "I wish that my master were with the prophet who is in Samaria! Then he would cure him of his leprosy," she spoke with such a clear conviction that Naaman's wife felt she simply had to share it with her husband.

Far from dismissing this idea which had begun to circulate in the home, Naaman reported it to the king. That even the king took it seriously, with full credence, is testimony to the impact the young girl's statement had made. Soon the king was writing a letter addressed to his counterpart in the girl's country, the land of Israel. And so it was, that one day soon after, armed with that letter of introduction and request from the king, the famous captain set off on what was his most important mission yet – the search for a cure for his killer disease.

At first, things didn't appear to be going well. The king of Israel took offence at the letter, suspecting it was some kind of scheme to engineer a quarrel. How could he fulfil such an impossible request; and so how could he avoid giving offence by his refusal or failure. Fortunately, the prophet whom the young girl had so well remembered, heard of the king's visitor and the king's explosive reaction to what he considered a preposterous demand. Send him to me, he said. Naaman and his entourage soon rolled up at the prophet's door. Now things are progressing, Naaman might have thought, but his rising mood of optimism soon took a hit. There was no fanfare, no personal appearance by the holy man, no flourish of the hand: instead the man's servant came out to greet the famous warrior in what seemed like an off-hand way, and with some ridiculous talk about taking a bath in some muddy water.

Surely, the military commander was worthy of more respect than this! His pride having been stung with this insult, he turned his chariots towards home. But, cooler heads among his servants prevailed. 'Give it a try, what have you to lose', they counselled

him, 'after all you were prepared to try anything, to go to any
length to be cured – so why not try this?' Naaman would ever
after be grateful for such wise and courageous servants, and for
the fact that he did have second thoughts. He went down to the
Jordan river and bathed himself the specified seven times, finally
emerging with renewed skin. It was now time to return to Elisha,
the man of God, and express his deep gratitude ...

"When he returned to the man of God with all his company,
and came and stood before him, he said, "Behold now, I know
that there is no God in all the earth, but in Israel; so please take a
present from your servant now." But he said, "As the LORD
lives, before whom I stand, I will take nothing." And he urged
him to take it, but he refused. Naaman said, "If not, please let
your servant at least be given two mules' load of earth; for your
servant will no longer offer burnt offering nor will he sacrifice to
other gods, but to the LORD. In this matter may the LORD
pardon your servant: when my master goes into the house of
Rimmon to worship there, and he leans on my hand and I bow
myself in the house of Rimmon, when I bow myself in the house
of Rimmon, the LORD pardon your servant in this matter." He
said to him, "Go in peace." So he departed from him some
distance" (2 Kings 5:15-19).

Through Naaman, we learn that God's gifts, including the gift
of salvation, are not to be paid for. They are all of his grace which
comes to us through Christ and his cross (see Ephesians 2:8,9).
It's not altogether clear what the thinking of this new convert to
the God of Israel was. He admits he'd now have a troubled
conscience about all future worship in the house of the false god,
Rimmon. He asked for forgiveness in advance, for persisting in
doing what he now knew was a wrong thing to do. That, of
course, is a faulty notion, betraying an insincere repentance. We
simply can't bargain with God, and, in effect, say: 'Well, Lord, I

know your Word says 'A', but please understand the way it is with me, I'm afraid I'm going to have to do 'B', I'm sure however that you'll understand.'

Naaman, doubtless, considered himself to be trapped in an impossible situation. His duties of state, and his master's protection, demanded of him that he should accompany him in pagan worship, although his heart was no longer in it, for he now knew better. There are many today, who feel themselves to be compromised in a similar way. Family ties, political pressure, or logistical and geographical challenges, shape their choice of worship. They have learned the truth from God's Word, but cannot bring themselves for one reason or another to give full expression to it because of the situation they find themselves in.

Naaman was not of God's people, Israel, at that time. That racial distinction was significant then. It may seem, accordingly, that Elisha's response to Naaman's request conferred approval or at least toleration. Even if this should've been the case then, it wouldn't apply today, when Jew and Gentile are now on an equal footing (Ephesians 6), and all are equally under obligation, without exception, to give a full response to our Lord's biblically revealed teaching as to how we should serve and worship him.

We can't be sure what exactly Naaman planned to do with his two mules' load of earth when he got it back home. Was this to be a mere holy relic, or was he intending to build an earthen altar to the true God in that land – one that would be for his private devotions, cancelling out, as he thought, the times when he would be compelled to prostrate himself still before the idol of a false deity?

Whatever was the case, we dare not expect the Lord's indulgence if we ask for a two-mules'-load-of-earth-type compromise. Our own tailor-made work-arounds may satisfy our conscience but they don't in any way satisfy the high demands of God's Word. Some say 'God will understand that this is where I've always worshiped him' or 'it'd break my mother's heart if I were to leave the place where she and her mother before her have always worshiped God.' Naaman's recorded pragmatic attempt at a compromise cannot be taken as grounds for such thinking. The approach God endorses is a thorough-going one, as when he called Abraham out from his family and country to devote himself to the God of glory who'd freshly revealed himself to him: "Now the LORD said to Abram, "Go forth from your country, and from your relatives and from your father's house, to the land which I will show you ..." (Genesis 12:1).

Abraham's uncompromising obedience of faith is consistently endorsed as an example for us in the Bible. This is the standard God clearly expects, even to the breaking of family ties and past customs.

"The God of glory appeared to our father Abraham when he was in Mesopotamia, before he lived in Haran, and said to him, 'LEAVE YOUR COUNTRY AND YOUR RELATIVES, AND COME INTO THE LAND THAT I WILL SHOW YOU.' 'Then he left the land of the Chaldeans ..." (Acts 7:34).

"By faith Abraham, when he was called, obeyed by going out to a place which he was to receive for an inheritance; and he went out, not knowing where he was going" (Hebrews 11:8).

Will you also go?

CHAPTER NINE: BREAD AND WATER IN THE PROPHET'S HOUSE (JEROBOAM)

The young man came rushing through the door of the family home, his heart pounding with the news he had to tell. He'd seen some pretty amazing things that day. This young man was the son of a prophet, but his father was an old man now. I wonder, however, if in his father's ministry there'd ever been a day to compare with this one – a day in which he'd seen God's message spoken in power and supported by impressive evidences.

Let me tell you what the young man had seen that day. He's witnessed at first-hand a confrontation between the rebel northern king who was now at the head of the ten breakaway tribes of Israel, and confronting him, a solitary southern prophet. I said this king was a rebel, and Jeroboam, king of Israel, was certainly that. He'd rewritten Israel's God-given religious calendar and replaced it with one he'd made up all by himself. His agenda was political. And he wouldn't be the last powerful figure to abuse religious ideas for his own political ends.

On the day in question, it seems, the king – contrary to the instructions of God's Law – was personally engaged in offering sacrifice and incense upon the altar he'd made, when all of a sudden he was interrupted by the arrival of the man of God, the prophet from the south ...

"He cried against the altar by the word of the LORD, and said, 'O altar, altar, thus says the LORD, 'Behold, a son shall be born to the house of David, Josiah by name; and on you he shall sacrifice the priests of the high places who burn incense on you, and human bones shall be burned on you.' Then he gave a sign the same day, saying, "This is the sign which the LORD has spoken, 'Behold, the altar shall be split apart and the ashes which are on it shall be poured out'" (1 Kings 13:2-3).

Of course, the king reacted furiously against what he saw as unwelcome interference. He stretched out his hand, pointed at the prophet, and yelled 'seize him!' At once, two things happened. The most immediately obvious was that, as predicted, the altar split apart, pouring out its ashes. Perhaps it was a few seconds before it became clear that something else had happened. The king was still pointing at the prophet who had angered him. But his anger had turned to panic – because it was if his whole arm had frozen at full-stretch, and he couldn't regain control over it. Now the king was begging the man of God to pray to God that he might regain the normal use of his hand and arm again.

The prophet, the man of God, agreed to do so, and just as remarkably, normal function was restored to the king. Of course, the king's attitude changed once again, and he invited the man of God to return home with him to be refreshed and rewarded. Many a lesser man would have seized the opportunity with both hands, but our young friend who'd been witnessing all this, was surely impressed when he heard the man of God decline the royal invitation: "If you were to give me half your house I would not go with you, nor would I eat bread or drink water in this place. For so it was commanded me by the word of the LORD, saying, 'You shall eat no bread, nor drink water, nor return by the way which you came'" (1 King 13:8-9).

And having said that, he set out to return home by another route, rather than simply retracing his steps. It was at about this point in the story - as the young son of the prophet was retelling it back at home - that his father seemed to get excited and ask which way he'd seen the man of God go home. Then he asked for his donkey to be saddled, and off he rode in hot pursuit.

It wasn't long before, as he travelled, he came across a man sitting under an oak tree, enjoying its shade. He wondered if this could be the man of God, the one who'd refused the king's hospitality in obediently doing what God had asked him to do by returning without supper. Sure enough, the chap confirmed he was the prophet who'd come from Judah in the south and spoken against the wrong religious practices of the rebel northern king. What happened next is of real interest – look at these further words from 1 Kings 13:15-19:

"Then he said to him, 'Come home with me and eat bread.' He said, 'I cannot return with you, nor go with you, nor will I eat bread or drink water with you in this place. For a command came to me by the word of the LORD, 'You shall eat no bread, nor drink water there; do not return by going the way which you came.' He said to him, 'I also am a prophet like you, and an angel spoke to me by the word of the LORD, saying, 'Bring him back with you to your house, that he may eat bread and drink water.' But he lied to him. So he went back with him, and ate bread in his house and drank water."

All very reasonable you might think. How was the man of God to know that the old prophet was making it up to serve his own selfish purpose? It had been the man of God's intention to be obedient to God at the first, but now he'd been deceived. No big deal, in any case, surely? Well, we may think not, but here's the sequel, again as recorded in 1 Kings 13:

"Now it came about, as they were sitting down at the table, that the word of the LORD came to the prophet who had brought him back; and he cried to the man of God who came from Judah, saying, "Thus says the LORD, 'Because you have disobeyed the command of the LORD, and have not observed the commandment which the LORD your God commanded you, but have returned and eaten bread and drunk water in the place of which He said to you, 'Eat no bread and drink no water'; your body shall not come to the grave of your fathers.' It came about after he had eaten bread and after he had drunk, that he saddled the donkey for him, for the prophet whom he had brought back.

Now when he had gone, a lion met him on the way and killed him, and his body was thrown on the road, with the donkey standing beside it; the lion also was standing beside the body. And behold, men passed by and saw the body thrown on the road, and the lion standing beside the body; so they came and told it in the city where the old prophet lived. Now when the prophet who brought him back from the way heard it, he said, 'It is the man of God, who disobeyed the command of the LORD; therefore the LORD has given him to the lion, which has torn him and killed him, according to the word of the LORD which He spoke to him.'

Then he spoke to his sons, saying, 'Saddle the donkey for me.' And they saddled it. He went and found his body thrown on the road with the donkey and the lion standing beside the body; the lion had not eaten the body nor torn the donkey. So the prophet took up the body of the man of God and laid it on the donkey and brought it back, and he came to the city of the old prophet to mourn and to bury him. He laid his body in his own grave, and they mourned over him, saying, 'Alas, my brother!' After he had buried him, he spoke to his sons, saying, 'When I die, bury me in the grave in which the man of God is buried; lay my bones beside his bones. For the thing shall surely come to pass which he cried by the word of the LORD against the altar in Bethel and against all the houses of the high places which are in the cities of Samaria" (1 Kings 13:20-32).

And it did come to pass, in the time of reforming king Josiah as you can check for yourself by reading about it in 2 Kings 23. But the old prophet's bones weren't disturbed simply because he'd made sure they were laid beside those of the man of God. But what are we meant to learn from this? I think the first chapter of Paul's letter to the Galatians spells it out - Paul says there:

"I am amazed that you are so quickly deserting Him who called you by the grace of Christ, for a different gospel; which is really not another; only there are some who are disturbing you and want to distort the gospel of Christ. But even if we, or an angel from heaven, should preach to you a gospel contrary to what we have preached to you, he is to be accursed! For I would have you know, brethren, that the gospel which was preached by me is not according to man ... but I received it through a revelation of Jesus Christ" (Galatians 1:6-8,11).

Remember how the man of God had received a direct communication from God: which was to eat no supper. Then someone came to him who claimed to have a new, additional revelation from God. His mistake was to treat that as having the same authority as the direct, earlier message – even when it flatly contradicted what God had expressly said. Many others have made this same mistake over the 2,000 years of Christianity. World religions and pseudo-Christian cults have claimed to have a more recent revelation than what's found written in the Bible. We would do well to follow Paul's advice: even if an angel from heaven should give us a later revelation, we should reject it. In the Bible, God has spoken to us in his Son (see Hebrews 1:1-2).

The New Testament writings give us the teaching of Christ's apostles which they had directly from him. This is God's final word to us. Anything different, which claims to override it, must be rejected outright. We must take great care to obey as carefully as we can the written biblical commands of our Lord. No change or update of God's New Testament pattern for our service carries any divine endorsement. The good example of the earliest Christians is one of 'continuing steadfastly' (Acts 2:42).

CHAPTER TEN: A DIFFERENT KIND OF FIRE (NADAB AND ABIHU)

The day began like many others. The four brothers were already very familiar with their duties. They were Israel's first priests, the sons of Aaron, the high priest and brother to Moses, the nation's leader. Exclusive privileges belonged to their family. Through them, the people drew near to their God. They were, as always, busily occupied with officiating at the great altar in the courtyard surrounding the special tent known as the tabernacle. There they presided over the sacrifices which the people brought. There were four or five main categories of offerings and the priests had to know the different treatment and procedure for each type.

It was a responsible job, of that there was no doubt, for through their uncle Moses God had warned how departures from his detailed instructions would spell instant death. How could they forget this? Every day they were reminded of God's holiness as they looked to the back of the tent before which they served, and saw a column of cloud rising heavenwards. This cloud became a pillar of fire by night, and it was the highly visible token that their God was near, being in residence in that sacred tent before which they served.

But there's always the danger that time-consuming and detailed procedures which we don't fully understand can become tedious to us, tempting us into taking short-cuts. I well remember doing this many years ago with the cleansing routine for contact lenses. I was trying to minimise expense and save time, but I later paid for it when I suffered with corneal ulcers.

Two of the four brothers we talked about a moment ago perhaps felt like taking a shortcut – or just doing something different for a change. Their names were Nadab and Abihu. One day, they decided to try an experiment. God had specified that the only fire to be used in the service of his house was the fire which he himself had kindled from heaven on the great altar in the tabernacle courtyard.

But was it strictly necessary to use that fire, and only that fire? Well, experiment they did, and the result is recorded in Leviticus chapter 10: "Now Nadab and Abihu, the sons of Aaron, took their respective firepans, and after putting fire in them, placed incense on it and offered strange fire before the LORD, which He had not commanded them. And fire came out from the presence of the LORD and consumed them, and they died before the LORD" (Leviticus 10:1-2).

The fire they offered was 'strange' in that God had not authorized it. They didn't use the fire which God had kindled, the fire on the altar that was always kept burning. It was a fatal mistake, and for it they were consumed in summary judgement. Of course, and quite naturally, Aaron their father is deeply shocked. He at once begins to remonstrate with Moses, but ... "Moses said to Aaron, 'It is what the LORD spoke, saying, 'By those who come near Me I will be treated as holy, and before all the people I will be honored.' So Aaron, therefore, kept silent" (Leviticus 10:3).

I find that quite remarkable. Aaron kept silent. He closed his mouth. There was in fact nothing to be said. His sons had not treated God as holy: they hadn't honoured God, and they'd paid the terrible price for that as God's judgement fell on them. This was indeed what the LORD had spoken, and there was nothing more to be said. This is an example of what we read in Paul's letter to the Romans: "Now we know that whatever the Law says, it speaks to those who are under the Law, so that every mouth may be closed and all the world may become accountable to God ..." (Romans 3:19).

Today, many take it upon themselves to grumble at God and blame him for whatever happens. But this verse by Paul in Romans shows that in the final analysis all will be thoroughly convinced - the argument will be so conclusive that they'll have nothing to reply; all objections will be silenced. Some atheists have declared that when they get to the other side (should it exist) and stand before God (should he exist) they'll simply say: 'You never gave me enough evidence.' But they won't say that. Everyone's reaction in the coming day will be as Aaron's was back then - total silence.

Someone has imagined at the end of time: billions of people seated on a great plain before God's throne. Most shrank back from the brilliant light before them. But some groups near the front talked heatedly, not cringing with cringing shame - but with belligerence. "Can God judge us? How can He know about suffering?", snapped a young brunette. She ripped open a sleeve to reveal a tattooed number from a Nazi concentration camp. "We endured terror ... beatings ... torture ... death!"

In another group a Negro boy lowered his collar. "What about this?" he demanded, showing an ugly rope burn. "Lynched, for no crime but being black!" In another crowd there was a pregnant schoolgirl with sullen eyes: "Why should I suffer?" she murmured, "It wasn't my fault." Far out across the plain were hundreds of such groups. Each had a complaint against God for the evil and suffering He had permitted in His world.

How lucky God was to live in Heaven, where all was sweetness and light. Where there was no weeping or fear, no hunger or hatred. What did God know of all that man had been forced to endure in this world? For God leads a pretty sheltered life, they said.

So each of these groups sent forth their leader, chosen because he had suffered the most. A Jew, a negro, a person from Hiroshima, a horribly deformed arthritic, a thalidomide child. In the centre of the vast plain, they consulted with each other. At last they were ready to present their case. It was rather clever. Before God could be qualified to be their judge, He must endure what they had endured. Their decision was that God should be sentenced to live on earth as a man. Let him be born a Jew. Let the legitimacy of his birth be doubted. Give him a work so difficult that even his family will think him out of his mind.

Let him be betrayed by his closest friends. Let him face false charges, be tried by a prejudiced jury and convicted by a cowardly judge. Let him be tortured.

At the last, let him see what it means to be terribly alone. Then let him die so there can be no doubt he died. Let there be a great host of witnesses to verify it.

As each leader announced his portion of the sentence, loud murmurs of approval went up from the throng of people assembled. When the last had finished pronouncing sentence, there was a long silence. No one uttered a word ... for suddenly, all knew that God had already served His sentence.

If we come back again to Aaron and his surviving sons, we find that not only were they, too, silent before God's judgement, but they weren't even allowed to mourn for, or bury, their sons and brothers. But "Moses said to Aaron and to his sons Eleazar and Ithamar, 'Do not uncover your heads nor tear your clothes, so that you will not die and that He will not become wrathful against all the congregation. But your kinsmen, the whole house of Israel, shall bewail the burning which the LORD has brought about. You shall not even go out from the doorway of the tent of meeting, or you will die; for the LORD'S anointing oil is upon you.' So they did according to the word of Moses" (Leviticus 10:6-7).

Talk about a tough day at the office! But Moses even seemed to think that such a bad day might just be about to get worse. For, in despair, he discovered that Aaron hadn't followed standard procedures with the sin offering: "Moses searched carefully for the goat of the sin offering, and behold, it had been burned up! So he was angry with Aaron's surviving sons Eleazar and Ithamar, saying, "Why did you not eat the sin offering at the holy place?" (Leviticus 10:16-17). Without doubt Moses was afraid of further judgement from God.

"But Aaron spoke to Moses, '... When things like these happened to me, if I had eaten a sin offering today, would it have been good in the sight of the LORD?' When Moses heard that, it seemed good in his sight" (Leviticus 10:19-20). Surely we can sympathize with Aaron when he says 'when things like these happened to me' – it had been a really tough day to lose two of his sons like that. In the circumstances, he'd not felt that the holy privilege of eating the remains of the sin offering goat was one that the remaining members of his family could worthily enjoy. If only Nadab and Abihu had been as sensitive as that. Instead they'd conducted an unauthorised worship experiment on the presumption that it surely can't be all that important that we stick closely to God's instructions. One day, we too, will have to give an account to the Lord for what we've done with his detailed commandments. Will we have anything to say?

CHAPTER ELEVEN: A SECOND EPHOD (GIDEON)

It was hot work in the winepress. However, the young man known as Gideon was not, as you might expect, treading on the grapes to extract their juice, but – most unusually – instead of grapes there was wheat strewn all over the floor and Gideon was beating it in order to thresh it to remove the grain from the useless chaff. I'm guessing it must have been a small harvest. How, in this undercover place, he was intending to fully remove the chaff, I don't know – for the normal practice was to do this on a raised, flat, windswept spot where the wind would blow away the lighter chaff, leaving the heavier grain behind.

But Gideon was in fact being resourceful, for these difficult times called for unusual methods. Ever since their enemy, the people who were known as the Midianites, had gained the upper hand, and grown accustomed to making raids into Israel's territory and to helping themselves to a free harvest, Gideon had developed this subtle technique.

Perhaps this might seem to us as the first indication that God was moving in Gideon's young life. Here was someone who wasn't willing to accept the inevitable. He was trying to save some of the harvest at least for his people's own use. But, even with this spirit of resistance, Gideon could never have expected the visitor he received. He was sitting in the shade of the old oak tree in Gideon's hometown of Ophrah while Gideon was secretly beating out the wheat. But just who was he? You'd have been forgiven for suspecting it was an angel or even a man – but soon

Gideon would have clear evidence that this was a very remarkable appearance of God in temporary human form.

When the figure addressed Gideon as a 'valiant warrior' it's possible that Gideon checked if there was anyone standing directly behind him, because that's not how he saw himself. And when Gideon was told that the Lord was with him, he shot back the same question that still haunts people today – if God is with us, then how come all these bad things are happening to us? Surely, Gideon must have thought, the reality is that God has abandoned us to the enemy Midianites? But the visitor was insistent that Gideon would be the one to deliver Israel from the enemy.

And so in that extraordinary way Gideon was given his commission. Gideon's response was to build an altar to the Lord who had appeared to him, and to destroy his father's pagan altar. The fact that his father had a pagan altar was so typical of the ways things were at that time and symptomatic of why God's people were under the thumb of their enemies. But Gideon was so afraid to make this stand that he had to do it secretly at night. But, at least he did it. He took that first small step of obedience.

The next challenge was a lot greater, and it came soon: "Then all the Midianites and the Amalekites and the sons of the east assembled themselves; and they crossed over and camped in the valley of Jezreel. So the Spirit of the LORD came upon Gideon; and he blew a trumpet, and the Abiezrites were called together to follow him" (Judges 6:33-34).

Famously, Gideon double-checked with God that God would truly help him as he'd promised (read Judges 6:36-40). God graciously gave Gideon the reassurances he asked for, but he did put Gideon's faith and obedience to the test by restricting his army right down to only 300 men. But the Lord, as promised, fought for his people, and the enemy were put to flight.

While in pursuit, Gideon called on others from the 12 tribes of Israel to join in the chase so as to ensure a total victory (Judges 7:24). This brought some criticism of Gideon's leadership – as to why he'd not called on them earlier – but Gideon showed leadership by handling it both diplomatically (Judges 8:3) and with firmness (Judges 8:16). When it was clear to all that a comprehensive victory had been secured ...

"Then the men of Israel said to Gideon, 'Rule over us, both you and your son, also your son's son, for you have delivered us from the hand of Midian.' But Gideon said to them, 'I will not rule over you, nor shall my son rule over you; the LORD shall rule over you.' Yet Gideon said to them, 'I would request of you, that each of you give me an earring from his spoil.' (For they had gold earrings, because they were Ishmaelites.) They said, 'We will surely give them.' So they spread out a garment, and every one of them threw an earring there from his spoil ... Gideon made it into an ephod, and placed it in his city, Ophrah, and all Israel played the harlot with it there, so that it became a snare to Gideon and his household.

Then Jerubbaal the son of Joash went and lived in his own house ... And Gideon the son of Joash died at a ripe old age and was buried in the tomb of his father Joash, in Ophrah of the Abiezrites. Then it came about, as soon as Gideon was dead, that the sons of Israel again played the harlot with the Baals, and made Baal-berith their god. Thus the sons of Israel did not remember the LORD their God, who had delivered them from the hands of all their enemies on every side; nor did they show kindness to the household of Jerubbaal (that is, Gideon) in accord with all the good that he had done to Israel" (Judges 8:22-25, 27,29, 32-35).

The ephod was that particular part of the high priest's clothing which was worn when the priest inquired of God. It seems that Gideon being now the civil ruler, desired to have an ephod of his own, kept in his own city, perhaps to be worn by the priest whenever Gideon might summon him to inquire of the Lord for him. Gideon's strained relations with the tribe of Ephraim probably made him unwilling to travel to Shiloh to consult the high priest stationed there.

Now this is the ending to the story I want to concentrate on. By now, we're not surprised by Gideon's humility. He was never someone who was seeking great things for himself. So he declined the offer of becoming, in effect, Israel's king and the start of a ruling dynasty. The curious thing is what he did ask for, and the golden ephod which he made from the donated earrings. Let's clarify again that the ephod was the shoulder-dress of the high priest. It was an item of clothing not unlike a vest, in the way a sports vest is worn over a top in order to differentiate between competing teams. By means of the ephod and what was attached to it and what it contained – by such means the priest obtained answers from God as to what his will was in a particular matter when, for example, he was consulted (later in history) by the king.

So why did Gideon make himself an ephod? Previously, he's built an altar and at God's instruction he'd even conducted a sacrifice upon it. Was Gideon now trying to take over more of the duties of the priest – this time without God's consent? And if so, was this a reflection on the disrepute into which the official high-priesthood in Israel at the time had fallen? Although Gideon had declined official status as a king-like leader, might he have been nevertheless equipping himself with this object as an oracle – so to be able to deal with hard cases in a continuing default role as the people's civil ruler?

And again, if so, with some biblical justification, we may ask if there was any sense in which he wished in this way to be less dependent on having to consult the ephod-wearing priest – especially since that priest was located within the territory of Ephraim from which quarter heavy criticism had come to Gideon during the battle? However, whether intentionally or not (and it seems unlikely that it was intentional based on verse 33) Gideon was, sadly, laying the foundation for a return to the confused mixture of belief in the true God mixed with the practice of paganism. And this is in fact what happened after his death when the ephod he made came to be treated as an idol.

Thinking of ourselves now: do we long – or find it more convenient - to personally take on a role which God's Word doesn't intend for, or even permit, us to fulfil (e.g. Romans 12-13)? Do we sacrifice in some respects our understanding of what God's Word asks us to do, simply because to go where it's being carried out fully would involve us meeting with people we'd frankly rather not meet? How often do you hear of breakaway groups forming because of unresolved church tensions?

In how many ways, I wonder, are we guilty today – as it would seem Gideon was in his day - of making pragmatic or so-called politically correct decisions which clearly compromise the original purity of God's Word? Are there not times (for example in the areas of gender and marriage) when the Word of God is set aside altogether in favour of the popular vote? Let's be careful we don't muddy the water for others, as Gideon did. His actions, which were at best unwise, paved the way for the people to sin.

CHAPTER TWELVE: A PIECE OF BRASS (HEZEKIAH)

Things were not going well. You've been there too - some place, sometime in your life when things were not working out like you expected. It was a not untypical day in the life of Moses, the leader who'd led the Israelites out of Egypt's slavery. The story of the Old Testament is very largely the story of the people of Israel whom God rescued from Egyptian slavery. God had promised his people that a land of plenty lay ahead. But it was taking time to get there. That was deliberate, of course. God's plan was to humble his people, and test them, to expose all that was in their heart (Deuteronomy 8:2). So, he deliberately allowed his people to grow hungry, as part of the way in which he disciplined them to test if they would walk in his ways and reverence him.

On this particular day, while on a lengthy detour by way of the Red Sea around the land of Edom, the people had just about had enough. Impatient because of the journey, they complained against God and Moses. To begin with, they moaned about the fact there was no food and no water, and so of course, as they saw it, they were going to die in the desert. They'd have been better off back in Egypt. The reality was that God was providing bread for them each day, but they didn't like its taste, and they weren't satisfied.

So, as we said, things weren't going well. But it was going to get worse, for we read in Numbers that: "The LORD sent fiery serpents among the people and they bit the people, so that many people of Israel died. So the people came to Moses and said, 'We have sinned, because we have spoken against the LORD and you; intercede with the LORD, that He may remove the serpents from us.' And Moses interceded for the people. Then the LORD said to Moses, 'Make a fiery serpent, and set it on a standard; and it shall come about, that everyone who is bitten, when he looks at it, he will live.' And Moses made a bronze serpent and set it on the standard; and it came about, that if a serpent bit any man, when he looked to the bronze serpent, he lived" (Numbers 21:6-9).

This, you may remember, is the incident referred to in John's Gospel, chapter 3: "As Moses lifted up the serpent in the wilderness, even so must the Son of Man be lifted up; so that whoever believes will in Him have eternal life. For God so loved the world, that He gave His only begotten Son, that whoever believes in Him shall not perish, but have eternal life" (John 3:14-16).

The snake on the stake, or the serpent on the pole, to be looked at in faith, was a picture of a greater salvation all those years later. It pictured the time when Jesus Christ, God's son, hung suspended on the cross to pay the price some 2000 years ago of all our human rebellion against God. For everyone today the Christian message is again one of 'look and live': meaning a look in faith to the Christ of the cross brings the ultimate healing of forgiveness by God into our lives. But let's get back to the days of Moses ...

After this incident involving the snake being raised on a pole, life continued, and the journey to the Promised Land went on. But whatever happened, we might ask, to that snake which Moses had made out of brass? Well, what we do know is that the Israelites kept it. You might think that the preservation of this relic might, like the pot of manna and Aaron's rod, have remained an instructive monument of God's goodness and mercy to the Israelites in the wilderness. Was that why they kept it? This brazen serpent Moses made in the desert, which had been brought by the children of Israel even into the land of Canaan itself, was it intended that it should always be kept as a memorial of the gracious miracle God had worked when those bitten had simply and obediently looked to it?

I very much doubt that superstitious reverence had been paid to it ever since the time of Moses, for such idolatry surely wouldn't have been tolerated by Asa or Jehoshaphat had they been aware of such foolishness. No, more likely, the introduction of the practice of reverencing the image of the brass serpent dates from of an ungodly king like Ahaz. Did some people later come to misunderstand, or wrongly recall, what'd happened in the desert in the time of Moses. After all, serpent-worship, however revolting it may appear, was far from an uncommon form of idolatry in the ancient world; and it would get an easier reception in Israel because of the fact that many of the neighbouring nations, such as the Egyptians and Phoenicians, worshiped idol gods in the form of serpents as emblems of health and immortality.

We even can't discount the fact that this bronze snake image might have been regarded as a sacred relic (something to be venerated) simply because it had been made by Moses. And generation after generation may have heard some distorted story of how a supernatural power in the snake itself had made it a means of healing the Israelites. If so, later generations could easily have come to imagine that it might be of some service to them too in any time of trouble.

If it was in the time of king Ahaz that this relic had begun to be misused then such misuse didn't last long, for we read of how when Hezekiah the son of Ahaz king of Judah became king: "He was twenty-five years old when he became king, and he reigned

twenty-nine years in Jerusalem; and his mother's name was Abi
the daughter of Zechariah. He did right in the sight of the
LORD, according to all that his father David had done. He
removed the high places and broke down the sacred pillars and
cut down the Asherah. He also broke in pieces the bronze
serpent that Moses had made, for until those days the sons of
Israel burned incense to it; and it was called Nehushtan. He
trusted in the LORD, the God of Israel; so that after him there
was none like him among all the kings of Judah, nor among those
who were before him. For he clung to the LORD; he did not
depart from following Him, but kept His commandments, which
the LORD had commanded Moses" (2 Kings 18:2-6).

We're told there that good king Hezekiah broke in pieces the
brazen serpent. It surely took courage to destroy what had
become the object of idolatrous worship. He even went so far as
to call it 'Nehushtan'. In some parts of the English-speaking
world today, we hear of someone who 'calls a spade a spade.' This
is usually said as a compliment. It describes someone who talks
plainly. Such a man tells it as it truly is. It seems like Hezekiah
was that kind of man. In a day when people were reverencing this
relic and probably attributing supernatural powers to it,
Hezekiah called it a piece of brass, for that's all it was. He saw
how they'd been ensnared by it, and drawn into idolatry to it, and
by way of contempt, he called it by this name, 'Nehushtan',
which literally just means 'a thing of brass'. Obviously, he was
suggesting that it was only a mere piece of brass – and absolutely
with no divinity in it. Such a thing could be of no service to the
people in divine things; and, so that it would no longer be a snare
to them, he broke it into pieces.

Well done, Hezekiah! He was a true reformer. It's so easy – in
religious matters, as in any other field – to see things the way
everyone else around us does. Hezekiah bucked that trend. He

was a man of strong personal convictions and outstanding faith
in God, which was anchored in God's Word, for he clung to the
Lord and kept his commandments.

There are all sorts of religious ideas that get handed down
from past generations. Even to this day, many revere holy relics of
one sort or another. When, towards the close of the first century,
the Apostle John signed off his first letter saying, 'Guard
yourselves from idols', I don't suppose for a moment he was
thinking of brazen images. If the preceding content of his letter is
anything to go by, his concern at that time was focused on faulty
mental images of God – and especially of God's Son, Jesus Christ.
It seems some were trying to split his personality: to say the man
Jesus only possessed deity in some temporary degree. Other faulty
thinking in the early days of Christianity, which the Apostle Paul
battled against, was the persistently attractive human notion that
we can and must contribute to our own salvation by the
performance of certain time-honoured religious rituals. Much
nearer to our own times, another reformer, Luther, exposed the
biblical error in that kind of thinking. He discovered from
Romans 1:17 that we are made right with God through faith
alone, and not by our own working.

Hezekiah's father, and Hezekiah's own generation, had got it
wrong. Like others God has used to preserve truth, Hezekiah was
prepared if necessary to be in a minority of one – so long as God
was with him. God doesn't ask us to follow other people's pattern
of behaviour, but to follow the pattern for serving him which is
found in the Bible. Hezekiah benchmarked his life against that of
his ancestor David, and for us our model is David's greater son,
Jesus.

CHAPTER THIRTEEN: SEVEN LOCKS OF HAIR (SAMSON)

The story of Samson is one which has perhaps had more than its fair share of exposure at the hands of film directors and song-writers. The reason is obvious enough - the story line provides scope for imaginative embellishments featuring a flawed hero as the male lead with the kind of love interest that appeals so much to Hollywood. But the biblical Samson was to be a Nazirite – that's someone under a special vow of dedication to God. The conditions of this vow are spelled out in the fourth book of Moses, the Old Testament book of Numbers. The fact that Samson was to be a Nazirite must be important because it's repeated several times in the early part of his story (Judges 13:7,13-14).

Let's remind ourselves how the news of Samson's special life of dedication was broken to his parents-to-be, along with the news of his impending birth in Judges 13:5: "For behold, you shall conceive and give birth to a son, and no razor shall come upon his head, for the boy shall be a Nazirite to God from the womb; and he shall begin to deliver Israel from the hands of the Philistines." This is how the Nazirite vow, which Samson was to follow, is described in the Bible book of Numbers: 'All the days of his vow of separation no razor shall pass over his head. He shall be holy until the days are fulfilled for which he separated himself to the LORD; he shall let the locks of hair on his head grow long" (Numbers 6:5).

Long, uncut hair was to become the most obvious sign of any Nazirite's total commitment and subjection to God. Samson's great strength was not magically produced by his long hair, of course. The secret of his strength lay in God – through his faithfulness to his vow – a faithfulness symbolized by his uncut hair. It's interesting that in First Corinthians chapter 11, the apostle Paul, in verse 14, cites nature as teaching us that if a man has long hair then it's a dishonour to him. Certainly, then, a man with a Nazirite vow was not seeking his own honour, but was focusing on living for the honour of God. He denied himself, while living as one who was committed to a higher 'law'.

A Swiss lady once advertised for a chauffeur and received three job applications. She interviewed them individually, each time asking the same question: "How close to a precipice could you drive and still be safe?" The first assured her that he could come within 15 centimeters in complete safety. The second applicant boasted that he could let his outer wheel run on the edge and still have nothing to worry about. The third and last candidate admitted that he didn't know, but that he'd simply prefer to keep as far away as possible. Needless to say, he got the job! In those terms, Samson was someone who drove too close to the edge of temptation. The result was he went over the edge. Judges chapter 6 tells us how it happened:

"After this it came about that he loved a woman in the valley of Sorek, whose name was Delilah. The lords of the Philistines came up to her and said to her, "Entice him, and see where his great strength lies and how we may overpower him that we may bind him to afflict him. Then we will each give you eleven hundred pieces of silver." So Delilah said to Samson, "Please tell me where your great strength is and how you may be bound to afflict you" (Judges 16:4-6).

That was hardly subtle, was it? But it appears that Samson was so complacent that he didn't take it seriously. He toyed with her, spinning stories about how his strength could be overcome by ropes. Then, it seems, he enjoyed the game of snapping those ropes, in an impressive demonstration of strength. But then ...

"... Delilah said to Samson, 'Up to now you have deceived me and told me lies; tell me how you may be bound.' And he said to her, 'If you weave the seven locks of my hair with the web and fasten it with a pin, then I will become weak and be like any other man.' So while he slept, Delilah took the seven locks of his hair and wove them into the web. And she fastened it with the pin and said to him, 'The Philistines are upon you, Samson!' But he awoke from his sleep and pulled out the pin of the loom and the web. Then she said to him, 'How can you say, "I love you," when your heart is not with me? You have deceived me these three times and have not told me where your great strength is.' It came about when she pressed him daily with her words and urged him, that his soul was annoyed to death.

So he told her all that was in his heart and said to her, 'A razor has never come on my head, for I have been a Nazirite to God from my mother's womb. If I am shaved, then my strength will leave me and I will become weak and be like any other man.' When Delilah saw that he had told her all that was in his heart, she sent and called the lords of the Philistines, saying, 'Come up once more, for he has told me all that is in his heart.' Then the lords of the Philistines came up to her and brought the money in their hands. She made him sleep on her knees, and called for a man and had him shave off the seven locks of his hair. Then she began to afflict him, and his strength left him.

She said, 'The Philistines are upon you, Samson!' And he awoke from his sleep and said, 'I will go out as at other times and shake myself free.' But he did not know that the LORD had departed from him. Then the Philistines seized him and gouged out his eyes; and they brought him down to Gaza and bound him with bronze chains, and he was a grinder in the prison" (Judges 16:13-21).

What a disaster! And one which seemed so unnecessary. But Satan knew where Samson was weak, just as he also knows where each one of us is weak. As Samson began to make reference to his hair, he was beginning to get close to the edge – and to toy with the serious matter of his consecration, as symbolized by his long hair. Our dedication to the Lord is not something to be treated lightly. In this way, Samson had ceased to be faithful to God, and so the strength he'd had from God was no longer available as before.

The charms of a woman who had no interest in God, and who was in league with the enemy of God's people, had taken him captive. Samson had been side-tracked and neutralized. Satan had succeeded in moving him away from where he was needed. The Lord also wants each of us to be strong and to remain so for him. The Apostle Paul wrote to Timothy: "... be strong in the grace that is in Christ Jesus. The things which you have heard from me ... entrust these to faithful men who will be able to teach others also ... Suffer hardship with me, as a good soldier of Christ Jesus. No soldier in active service entangles himself in the affairs of everyday life" (2 Timothy 2:1-4).

Samson lost his strength for God by losing his faithfulness through getting tangled up in a relationship that was not God's will for him. It may, of course, be other things for us – perhaps legitimate business interests that begin to take over our life and draw us away from being faithful with our time commitment and energies for the Lord's priority things in our life. Slowly but surely, the strength of our testimony and the vibrancy of our Christian life and witness is neutralized. The antidote is to: "Be diligent to present yourself approved to God as a workman who does not need to be ashamed, accurately handling the word of truth. But avoid worldly and empty chatter, for it will lead to further ungodliness ..." (2 Timothy 2:15-16).

After mentioning some by name who had "gone astray from the truth" Paul continues by saying: "... flee from youthful lusts and pursue righteousness, faith, love and peace, with those who call on the Lord from a pure heart ... with gentleness correcting those who are in opposition, if perhaps God may grant them repentance leading to the knowledge of the truth, and they may come to their senses and escape from the snare of the devil, having been held captive by him to do his will" (2 Timothy 2:22,25-26).

May we stay strong in and for the truth, not allowing ourselves to be ensnared, entangled or in any way taken captive to do the Devil's will – but by maintaining our faithfulness, may we do God's will still. May we be strengthened by God's grace to stay faithful.

CHAPTER FOURTEEN: THE BLEATING OF SHEEP (SAUL)

Samuel would never forget the first time he ever set eyes on Saul. The day before that meeting God had spoken to the prophet Samuel and told him he was going to send to him, on the very next day in fact, the future king of Israel. And when Saul came and approached Samuel in the city gate, he really did look every bit the kind of prince you might expect: for he was tall and handsome. But Samuel, would, I think, be just as impressed by his attitude. For Saul was a humble young man, one who freely confessed his lowly origins (see 1 Samuel 9:21).

Before they parted company on that first meeting, Samuel had anointed Saul with oil, which was the ritual that marked out Saul as the one who was going to be future king. But when the actual day came for Saul to be announced as king and presented to the people, no-one could find him. Far from being someone to promote himself, he appeared to be very reluctant to take on such a responsibility.

The first test of his leadership came early on in his reign when he met the challenge of rescuing a besieged city. At that time there were those who thought others who'd doubted Saul should be put to death, but Saul refused to allow that to happen. Again that was good. But then came a bigger test when ...

"... the Philistines assembled to fight with Israel ... the men of Israel saw that they were in a strait (for the people were hard-pressed), then the people hid themselves in caves, in thickets, in cliffs, in cellars, and in pits. Also some of the Hebrews crossed the

Jordan into the land of Gad and Gilead. But as for Saul, he was still in Gilgal, and all the people followed him trembling. Now he waited seven days, according to the appointed time set by Samuel, but Samuel did not come to Gilgal; and the people were scattering from him. So Saul said, 'Bring to me the burnt offering and the peace offerings.' And he offered the burnt offering.

As soon as he finished offering the burnt offering, behold, Samuel came; and Saul went out to meet him and to greet him. But Samuel said, 'What have you done?' And Saul said, 'Because I saw that the people were scattering from me, and that you did not come within the appointed days, and that the Philistines were assembling at Michmash, therefore I said, "Now the Philistines will come down against me at Gilgal, and I have not asked the favor of the LORD." So I forced myself and offered the burnt offering.' Samuel said to Saul, 'You have acted foolishly; you have not kept the commandment of the LORD your God, which He commanded you, for now the LORD would have established your kingdom over Israel forever. But now your kingdom shall not endure'" (1 Samuel 13:5-14).

This was the first of two distinct instances in which Saul disobeyed the Lord. On that first occasion, Saul seems to have been driven by fear and impatience. The next time he disobeyed is found two chapters later in First Samuel chapter 15 when God told him through Samuel: '"... I will punish Amalek for what he did to Israel, how he set himself against him on the way while he was coming up from Egypt. Now go and strike Amalek and utterly destroy all that he has, and do not spare him; but put to death both man and woman, child and infant, ox and sheep, camel and donkey' ... Saul came to the city of Amalek and set an ambush in the valley ... So Saul defeated the Amalekites, from Havilah as you go to Shur, which is east of Egypt" (1 Samuel 15:2-3,5,7).

At this point we're thinking 'well done, Saul - you seem to have got it right this time.' And sure enough, when Samuel comes to see Saul after the battle, Saul says to him: 'I have carried out the command of the LORD' (1 Samuel 15:13). But then Samuel says, 'What then is this bleating of the sheep in my ears ...?' You see, what had really happened was that Saul had "captured Agag the king of the Amalekites alive, and utterly destroyed all the people with the edge of the sword. But Saul and the people spared Agag and the best of the sheep, the oxen, the fatlings, the lambs, and all that was good, and were not willing to destroy them utterly; but everything despised and worthless, that they utterly destroyed" (1 Samuel 15:8-9).

With that second act of sinful disobedience by Saul, the Lord withdrew his favour. Samuel informs Saul that God has now rejected him from being king. But before Samuel finally turned away, for he never saw him again, he gave Saul this explanation of why God had rejected him. He said, "Is it not true, though you were little in your own eyes, you were made the head of the tribes of Israel? And the LORD anointed you king over Israel, and the LORD sent you on a mission, and said, 'Go and utterly destroy the sinners, the Amalekites, and fight against them until they are exterminated.' Why then did you not obey the voice of the LORD, but rushed upon the spoil and did what was evil in the sight of the LORD?' Then Saul said to Samuel, 'I did obey the voice of the LORD, and went on the mission on which the LORD sent me, and have brought back Agag the king of Amalek, and have utterly destroyed the Amalekites. But the people took some of the spoil, sheep and oxen, the choicest of the things devoted to destruction, to sacrifice to the LORD your God at Gilgal.' Samuel said, "Has the LORD as much delight in burnt offerings and sacrifices as in obeying the voice of the LORD? Behold, to obey is better than sacrifice ..." (1 Samuel 15:15-22).

Notice how Saul first protests his innocence. Then he blames the people. Finally, he adds the gloss that the intention was good: it was to offer the plunder as sacrifices to God. Even if we take this at face value, what it really is saying is that Saul – and perhaps the people – thought they could improve on God's command! God had said take absolutely no plunder, destroy it all totally (this was because God remembered the treachery of this same enemy people and what they'd done against Israel shortly after God had brought Israel up out of Egypt). So it was a case of take no prisoners, no plunder of people or livestock – but destroy everything, absolutely everything. God had made this very clear, but Saul had decided that rather than doing exactly that, they'd save the very best things to sacrifice them to God. So Saul appeared to think he'd had a better idea than God!

This reminds me of an illustration I once heard someone share during a Bible study many years ago. He told of a father who told his young daughter on no account ever to cross the busy main road. Sometime later, on the occasion of his birthday, he was delighted to receive a birthday gift from his daughter. However, his joy was tempered when he realized that she'd defied his instruction and crossed the main road to buy that present in the shop on the opposite side of the road. Now he has mixed emotions. For sure, there's delight at his daughter's thoughtfulness, but when he thinks of how she's gone against his word, it's a delight that's mingled with disappointment, hurt and even some anger.

The point of that story when I first heard it was to try to illustrate a situation like the one king Saul had got himself into – one in which a person does something to please God but in the process of doing it that person also commits an act of disobedience against God.

It may be tempting for us to do what we think will please God, but are we not actually doing what we please? It becomes hard to defend against that if the way we're claiming to serve God is contrary to the plain word of God as found in the Bible.

While not advocating any form of legalism, how could we begin to justify any course of action that departs from God's Word – whatever lofty motivation we may claim? As Paul says in 1 Corinthians 13:3: "And if I give all my possessions to feed the poor, and if I surrender my body to be burned, but do not have love, it profits me nothing." And what is the true, infallible test of our love for the Lord? Jesus answers in John 14:15, "If you love Me, you will keep My commandments."

CHAPTER FIFTEEN: LOVE FOR THE WORLD (DEMAS)

One of the most haunting passages among Paul's biblical letters is found in 2 Timothy 4:10 where he says: "Demas has forsaken me, having loved this present world, and has departed for Thessalonica." The apostle Paul was a 'people person.' He reached out to people, he mentored people, and if you study his prayers you'll notice he prayed for people – a lot. When one of those people, into whom he'd poured his life, turned back and deserted him, he really felt it. A real sense of desolation is reflected when he writes that "only Luke is with me" (2 Timothy 4:11).

We're not told where Demas was from. Some think that because he left Paul and went to Thessalonica this implies he was returning to his hometown. Maybe. If Demas was from Thessalonica, it'd be interesting to compare his life with that of Aristarchus because he was also from Thessalonica. Both may have been from a comfortable background and probably had some wealth, both were trained by the Apostle Paul, yet both men went in different spiritual directions.

Demas first appears in the Bible while in Rome during the Apostle Paul's first imprisonment (AD 60-62). In the last chapter of Colossians there's mention of at least eight believers, including Demas, who were there at that time with Paul – and all of whom were known to the churches in the Lycus Valley. Because of this, it would seem that Demas had been a visiting missionary to the Lycus Valley area.

Six of them send their greetings (Colossians 4:10-14), and Demas is listed with Luke and Epaphras (Colossians 4:12-14), separately from the three Jewish believers, Aristarchus, Mark, and Justus (Colossians 4:10-11) – so we take that as implying Demas was a Gentile. Five of Paul's companions, again including Demas, also send their personal greetings to Philemon at Colossae as well (Philemon vv. 23-24). Among the greetings to Philemon, Demas is included in the statement that describes him as a co-worker with Paul (Philemon 24). Perhaps he'd been a "close confidant of Paul, sharing the Apostle's vision of winning the world for God" (W. D. Thomas, 1983-84: p.179).

All of this would suggest he was someone who'd been a channel of God's blessing to others in his mission work alongside Paul. But now no longer. Paul wrote that Demas 'forsook him' (2 Timothy 4:10) – he'd let Paul down. How come? Because he "loved this present world." Paul doesn't tell us which aspect of the present world system Demas loved. He doesn't say if it was fame, fortune, or self-indulgence. Perhaps, he didn't want to embarrass his co-worker any further.

But also leaving this failure in Demas' life unspecified in this way meant it could serve as a broad, general warning to us. And we all need that warning - for remember how the Apostle John wrote to believers in Asia Minor: "Do not love the world or the things of the world ... For all that is in the world – the lust of the flesh, the lust of the eyes, and the pride of life – is not of the Father but is of the world" (1 John 2:15-17). The questions this raises are: "Are we living for time, or eternity?" and, "Are we living for this world, or God's kingdom?" The Christian should view the "world", as often used in the New Testament, as a moral and spiritual system which is designed to draw the believer in the Lord Jesus away from love for the Lord and any service for him (Galatians 1:4; 1 Timothy 6:17; Titus 2:12).

The world in its cultures, beliefs and values tries to draw the believer away from his or her love for the Lord in one of three ways. The first, the lust of the flesh, has to do with the gratification of the flesh (what makes us feel good physically). This includes sexual sins, gluttony, drug use and drunkenness. The second way is the lust of the eyes (whatever we see that we want to possess) - when the object we want is not ours but belongs to someone else, this comes down to covetousness. And the final category is the pride of life (what we want to be) – boasting about our potential accomplishments. Whatever the particular form of Demas' love for the world, it almost certainly fell into at least one of these three categories. Was Demas' issue more about desiring an easier lifestyle with more physical creature comforts, we might wonder?

Why Demas went to Thessalonica, and what he did there, isn't revealed in the Bible. One preacher who lived about AD 400 (John Chrysostom) suggested that "having loved his own ease and security from danger, [Demas] had chosen rather to live luxuriously at home, than to suffer hardships" with Paul (quoted in Oden 1989: p.176). If this is the case, the lure that Demas fell for was the lust of the flesh because he wanted an easy-going life without self-denial.

Polycarp in the 2nd century AD, wrote a letter in which he listed some early martyrs: Ignatius, Zosimus, Rufus, Paul and other apostles, and said that all these had not "run in vain" because they didn't "love this present world" (Polycarp to the Philippians 9:1, 2; LCL I: 295). Polycarp seems to be contrasting them to Demas when he says they didn't love this present world. He's implying, it seems, that Demas didn't want to be a martyr which is why he abandoned Paul in Rome before he was executed. Certainly, just before Paul's statement about Demas abandoning him, he's been talking about his own impending martyrdom (2 Timothy 4:6-8).

Whether or not Demas was running away from hardship and martyrdom, or just wanting more creature comforts, an easier-going life, with a bit of indulgence and luxury thrown in, it's clear we shouldn't try to copy the life of Demas. Instead, we should have an eternal perspective on life and not love this present world system that's out to draw us away from our devotion to the Lord and his Word. The hope of the Lord's return should change the way we live now. Paul, in contrast to Demas, lived his life in the light of the judgement-seat of Christ.

For sure, none of us is immune to loving this present world and leaving the Lord's work and the Lord's people (1 Corinthians 10:12). For us, it may be some kind of retreat into a comfort zone. Was Timothy tempted to take things easier, avoiding confrontation? Paul urged him to "suffer hardship as a good soldier of Christ." It is a battle. The world is subtle and is our foe. Its values are very different from those of God's Word. For example, society's idea of fairness can be radically different from what God's Word says. And we might be sensitive about being seen to be taking what's viewed as an extreme position; one, perhaps, that others may judge to be lacking in compassion.

This is just one way of "losing our life" for Christ's sake. Dying in this way is gain too. But how tempting it is to moderate our passion for God's Word! The desire to blend in and be accepted is strong. The world tells us that it considers being a Christian should be all about tolerance – including tolerance of things which God doesn't tolerate. The world today says we are all entitled to our personal view of what's true because there are no absolutes. They've all been abolished. But when Jesus said 'I am the Way' (to God), he was indeed saying that absolutely no one else is the way. Today, inclusiveness is a big issue. Worldly thinking argues that it's wrong to exclude anyone. But the Bible shows time and time again that sin excludes us from God's presence, and that truth is exclusive – of error.

"Jesus said to His disciples, "If anyone wishes to come after Me, he must deny himself, and take up his cross and follow Me. For whoever wishes to save his life will lose it; but whoever loses his life for My sake will find it. For what will it profit a man if he gains the whole world and forfeits his soul? Or what will a man give in exchange for his soul?" (Matthew 16:24-26).

Will we love the present world, will we love its applause, and so save our life in the here and now? Or will we lose our life for Jesus' sake by taking whatever the present consequences are of refusing to let the world squeeze us into its mould? It's better to be thought of as narrow-minded, a person of one book, as long as that one book is the unchanging Word of God!

FURTHER TITLES IN THIS SERIES

If you've enjoyed reading this book, first of all please consider taking a moment to leave a positive review on Amazon! Secondly, you may be interested to know that, at the date of the publishing of this book, the Search For Truth library now stands at almost fifty titles; each contains excellent reading material in a down-to-earth and conversational style, covering a wide range of topics from Bible character studies, theme studies, book studies, apologetics, prophecy, Christian living and more. The simplest way to access this material for purchase is by visiting Brian's Amazon author page:

Amazon.com: http://amzn.to/1u7rzIA

Amazon.co.uk: http://amzn.to/YZt5zC

Alternatively, the books can also be found simply by searching for the specific title or "Search For Truth Series" on Amazon. Paperback versions can also be purchased from Hayes Press at www.hayespress.org.

Take a look at some of the books in the library below:

PAPERBACK EDITIONS

The Supremacy of Christ

Nothing But Christ Crucified: First Corinthians

Christianity 101: 7 Bible Basics

Nights of Old: Bible Stories of God at Work

Pure Milk: Nurturing the New Life in Jesus

Once Saved, Always Saved? The Reality of Eternal Salvation

Jesus: What Does the Bible Really Say?

The Tabernacle: God's House of Shadows

A Legacy of Kings: Israel's Chequered History

Healthy Churches: God's Bible Blueprint for Growth

Hope for Humanity: God's Fix for a Broken World

Fencepost Turtles: People Placed by God

Minor Prophets – Major Issues

Tribes and Tribulations – Israel's Predicted Personalities

Bible Answers to Listeners' Questions

One People for God Omnibus

Kings, Tribes and Prophets Omnibus

God – His Glory, His Building, His Son Omnibus

Decoding Daniel: Deciphering Bible Prophecy

All these titles are also available in Kindle e-book format from Amazon.

EBOOK EDITIONS

Apologetics

Overcoming Objections to Christian Faith

Windows to Faith

Turning the World Upside Down

An Unchanging God?

Life, the Universe and Ultimate Answers

Bible Answers for Big Questions

Books of the Bible

Double Vision – The Insights of Isaiah

Unlocking Hebrews

James – The Epistle of Straw

The Visions of Zechariah

Experiencing God in Ephesians

Daniel Decoded: Deciphering Old Testament Prophecy

Bible Character Studies

Abraham – Friend of God

About The Bush – The Life of Moses

After God's Own Heart: The Life of David

Samson: A Type of Christ

Esther: A Date with Destiny

Discipleship

Praying with Paul

The Way: New Testament Discipleship

Power Outage: Christianity Unplugged

Closer Than a Brother – Christian Friendship

No Compromise!

Jesus Christ

Five Women and a Baby: The Genealogy of Jesus

They Met at the Cross – Five Encounters with Jesus

Salt and the Sacrifice of Christ

The Last Words of Jesus

Jesus: Son Over God's House

General Topics

The Kingdom of God – Past, Present or Future?

God's Appointment Calendar: The Feasts of Jehovah

Seeds – A Potted Bible History

AWOL! Bible Deserters and Defectors

5 Sacred Solos – The Truths That The Reformation
Recovered

Trees of the Bible

Knowing God: Reflections on Psalm 23

The Glory of God

Living in God's House

Edge of Eternity – Approaching the End of Life

Tomorrow's Headlines – Bible Prophecy

The Five Loves of God

SEARCH FOR TRUTH RADIO BROADCASTS

Search for Truth Radio has been a ministry of the Churches of God (see www.churchesofgod.info) since 1978. Free Search for Truth podcasts can be listened to online or downloaded at four locations:

- At SFT's own dedicated podcast site: www.searchfortruth.podbean.com

- Via Itunes using the podcast app (search for 'Search For Truth')
- On the Churches of God website: (http://www.churchesofgod.info/search_for_truth_radi o_programmes.php)
- On the Transworld Radio website: (http://www.twr360.org/programs/ministry_id,103)

Alternatively, see below for details of digital and analogue radio timings.

Europe

Listen online at www.twr.org.uk/live.htm

SKY Digital Channel 0138 (11.390 GHz, ID 53555) and Freesat channel 790 and Freeview 733 in the **UK** - Saturday at 07.30 and Sunday at 06.45.

Malawi

Sunday on TWR Malawi FM Network at 06.45 UTC+2 (89.1 - 106.5 FM)

South East Asia

On Reach Beyond – Australia on Mondays 13.15 UTC, 25m band SW (15540 kHz.)

India

Tuesday and Friday on TWR Guam at 15.15, 19m band SW (15110 kHz.)

Thailand

Wednesday on TWR Guam at 08.50, 19m band SW (11965 kHz.)

Jamaica

Sunday on MegaJamz at 09.00, 98.7 FM

CONTACTING SEARCH FOR TRUTH

If you have enjoyed reading one of our books or listening to a radio broadcast, we would love to know about that, or answer any questions that you might have.

Contact us at:

SFT c/o Hayes, Press, The Barn, Flaxlands, Wootton Bassett, Swindon, Wiltshire SN4 8DY

P.O. Box 748, Ringwood, Victoria 3134, Australia

P.O. Box 70115, Chilomoni, Blantyre, Malawi

Web site: www.searchfortruth.org.uk

Email: sft@churchesofgod.info

Also, if you have enjoyed reading this book and/or others in the series, we would really appreciate it if you could just take a couple of minutes to leave a brief review on Amazon – it really is a very good way of spreading the word about our ministry – thanks and God bless!

Did you love *A Test of Commitment: 15 Challenges to Stimulate Your Devotion to Christ*? Then you should read *First Corinthians: Nothing But Christ Crucified* by Brian Johnston!

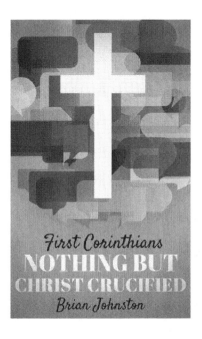

Bible teacher Brian Johnston unpacks the first letter of the apostle Paul to the Corinthians in this informative book, exploring such important topics as spiritual gifts, the body of Christ, headcoverings, the Breaking of Bread and the powerful wisdom of God in Christ crucified!

About the Author

Born and educated in Scotland, Brian worked as a government scientist until God called him into full-time Christian ministry on behalf of the Churches of God (www.churchesofgod.info). His voice has been heard on Search For Truth radio broadcasts for over 30 years during which time he has been an itinerant Bible teacher throughout the UK and Canada. His evangelical and missionary work outside the UK is primarily in Belgium and The Philippines. He is married to Rosemary, with a son and daughter.